2

Overcoming Digital Mess

Lionel Bolnet

Author and self-publisher:
Lionel Bolnet

Distributor:
www.lulu.com

All the practical cases mentioned are performed on Android, iOS or Windows. The concepts are transposable to Mac but with different approaches not detailed in this book.

Table of Contents

Definition

Digital mess is the chaotic situation in which our personal or professional computers have been in since the mid-90s: a confusing tree of misplaced and misnamed files. Even the owner of a PC or smartphone doesn't always know what files he or she has. Finding something specific quickly is mission impossible. As more and more files and devices accumulate, the digital mess gets worse every day.

However, there are solutions to make things clearer.

But tidying up for the sake of tidying up has no point. What this book offers you is to embark on **a sentimental journey to the** heart of your files, to consider them not as binary heaps but rather as **your digital biography**. Take your mind off the fact that files are administrative tools and see them now as **poignant testimonies of the** hectic life you, your children, your loved ones have lived. Instill happiness in your daily life thanks to the music you love, don't deny your pleasure in front of your favorite movie, relive the emotion of a wedding. You see, if you knew how to use your files, you wouldn't say "I don't remember", you wouldn't say "I saw that one day but where?

No matter how old you are, you're sure to have amassed a beautiful collection of digital memories just waiting to be sublimated to explode before your eyes!

Figure 1: Bringing up memories

"Your files are the pages of your digital biography".

Beyond the memories, you will see in this book how a well-organized file heritage allows you to gain autonomy, speed, productivity, confidence and even money savings.

History

The encounter between the general public and files dates back to around the 1980s, when the personal computer entered western homes.

On October 25, 1983, the computer company Microsoft released a word processing software called Word. The world then discovers a computer concept: the file. It is very difficult to give a date of invention of the computer file because it is a concept and not a tangible thing. It is easy to determine the invention date of the punch card (1728), the hard disk (1956) or the floppy disk (1967) but it is difficult to say when the concept of file was invented.

Still, from the 1980s onwards, the first users of office software (Word then Excel) began to have to store immaterial objects: files. The operating systems, mainly Mac and Windows, accompanied users towards this new feature by illustrating files with "icons" and organizing them in "trees".

At first, the task did not seem insurmountable. People had a handful of ".doc" or ".xls" files that they crammed into a single folder called "My Documents". The family computer was a simple successor to the typewriter. It was used to write a letter, a resume, and almost nothing more.

But, subsequently, other uses of computing have become more widespread. Around the year 2000, MP3 files made their appearance: they are files containing music. Then we discovered that (often pirated) movies could be stored in computers as ".avi", ".mp4" or ".mpg" files. Then, traditional photography gave way to digital pictures with ".jpg".

We also got to know ".pdf", ".gif" and ".ppt" which are respectively formatted documents, animated pictures and slide presentations.

More recently, even money is stored as files thanks to Bitcoins that are kept warm in ".dat".

The objects that can be printed with a 3D printer are ".3mf" files.

This trend of real-world conversation in digital files is called digitization. Everything goes or will go through it: music, videos, documents, pay slips, diplomas, money, bills, stamps, vouchers, plane tickets, train tickets, hotel reservations, leave their traditional medium to become files.

What are we going to do with this flood of files whose number and value is increasing day after day?

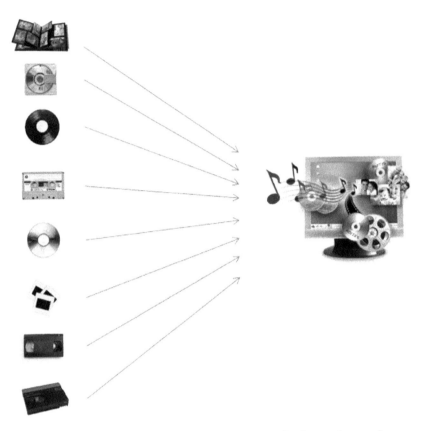

Figure 2: Most of the old storage methods are becoming obsolete and turning into computer files.

What this book offers you is a tour of the current techniques for storing files, but also passwords.

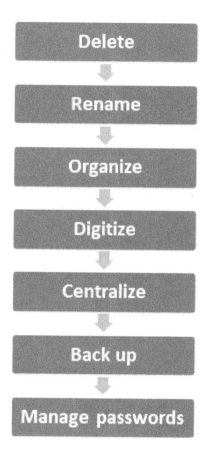

Figure 3: Sequence of actions

Delete

In both real life and digital life, a major component of the storage business is deletion.

Computers (Windows)

The first rule to get rid of digital mess is to delete unnecessary files. As PC users, our main bad habit is to keep everything.

Let's start with the "Downloads" folder for example. In most computers, the "Downloads" folder is the one that serves as a receptacle for files that are downloaded when surfing the web.

Theoretically, this folder should always be empty. It should be seen as a transit space: a place where files stay temporarily before reaching a permanent place or the trashcan.

For example, you buy a concert ticket online. At the end of the purchase, an e-mail is sent to you with an attachment, a PDF file. You download it in order to print it. From the same evening, you attend the concert. So why will this file stay for three years in your "Downloads" folder?

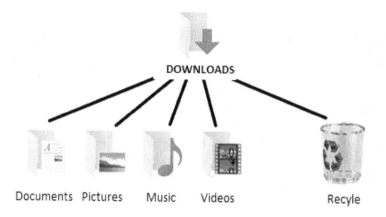

Figure 4: Downloaded files should go to a permanent folder or be deleted

There are other folders that should remain empty: "My Received Files" for example is a folder where some programs will tend to drop files received via instant messaging.

Finally, the most famous folder that should always be empty is "Desktop". In reality, the vast majority of Windows users put their files on the desktop. This is not what Microsoft expects, but it is a "desire path". A desired path is a bypass of the use of something by its users. For most people, the Desktop is the preferred location to drop files because:

- This is the first folder you see when you turn on a Windows computer,
- There is no risk of deletion,
- There is no need to navigate to find it.

The problem is that the Desktop is a factor increasing numerical mess because it is never tidy.

Figure 5: Example of an overloaded Windows desktop

The best thing to do is to position shortcuts on the desktop to the real folders that are Music, Videos, Pictures and Documents.

Deleting files takes time. You have to open each file one by one and ask yourself the question of their future usefulness. At this stage, it's more a question of human psychology than office automation: people always have a panic fear of deleting files. They say to themselves "what if one day I need this 2006 plane ticket invoice? "or "what if one day I start wanting to listen to that Bratisla Boys' music again"?

It's hard to admit that music you don't like can be removed because music, even when you don't like it, is an art form and you are unconsciously shocked to throw away a work of art. Even the file "McGyver_opening_theme.mp3".

For photos, it's the same problem: since we all have a camera in our pocket at all times, we accumulate a mountain of photographs, most of which are perfectly useless. Every day, this mountain grows by several megabytes, but few people tackle it. There are even duplicate and blurry photos but sorting them out would require spending a considerable number of hours in front of the computer.

The case of duplicates is easy to solve thanks to tools such as DupeGuru, a free duplicate detection/deletion software.

📖 🖥 *In the Tools chapter, a DupeGuru tutorial is available.*

Modernization of uses is also a factor in the deletion of files. For about fifteen years, MP3 files were the kings of music listening. We crammed thousands of them into our computers. Now this practice is being lost to legal listening platforms like Deezer or Spotify. So, if you are a customer of this kind of service, logically, you should take your "MP3" folder and throw it all in the trash, right?

The same question arises for "DivX", those 500 megabytes to 1 gigabyte video files that young people exchanged a lot at the beginning of the century. The legal retaliation has put a big stop to the spread of DivX. Video on demand (VOD) and subscription video on demand (S-VOD) such as Netflix, OCS or Amazon Prime Video offer their users the possibility to watch (almost) any movie or series without downloading it. Customers of these services can therefore discard their DivX video files.

Finally, when deleting a lot of files, don't forget to empty the Trash. You should avoid thinking that the files in the Trash don't take up any more space on the hard disk. On most personal computers, the Recycle Bin is the messiest folder. The Recycle Bin does not empty itself after 30 days.

When you have a laptop, you should try to have even fewer files than in a fixed computer because these devices are at increased risk of theft, loss or breakage. If you keep a lot of your files on a laptop, it is up to you to ensure that the confidential data on it cannot be exploited by a third party. Putting a password on the Windows session is essential but not sufficient because you just have to unscrew the computer, remove its hard disk or SSD, and then plug it into a USB port on another computer to read its contents.

Figure 6: Person unscrewing a laptop. Every time you leave your home with a laptop, you risk having it stolen and having someone do this manipulation to read its contents.

You must therefore think carefully and arbitrate between the need for confidentiality and the need for availability. The more files you put in your laptop, the more likely it is that they will fall into the wrong hands if you lose it.

In the following chapters, we will see where to store these files rather than in a laptop.

Smartphones

In the case of the smartphone, it is advisable to remain very careful: this object is portable so it runs a high risk of theft or loss. It is typically a "consumable" device: you buy it, you damage it, you drop it, you lose it, you buy it back in a cycle that lasts 12 to 18 months. When a smartphone is stolen, the files it contains are also stolen. This is why it is advisable to limit the contents of this kind of device by following the following risk chart:

Type of file	Confidentiality desired
MP3	None
APPLICATIONS	None
PHOTOS	High
VIDEOS	High
DOCUMENTS	Very high

MP3s and applications are files that can be accumulated at will in a smartphone because they are not confidential. On the other hand, photos and videos on a smartphone are usually intimate information. Finally, personal or professional documents such as PDFs of bills, scans of ID cards, pay slips, bank details or tax notices are too confidential to be stored in a smartphone. With these types of documents, a thief could usurp your identity and take out, for example, a consumer credit whose monthly payments would be deducted from your real bank account.

To avoid this, get into the habit of deleting the content of your smartphone. Do not consider your smartphone as a place to archive your life.

This chapter has talked a lot about files, but digital mess is also caused by programs, software and applications. It is advisable, especially on smartphones, to regularly delete applications that you never use. Unnecessary applications on a smartphone cause four major inconveniences:

- Slowing down of the device,
- Occupancy of storage space,
- Battery consumption,
- Risk of disclosures of personal data.

Whether on Android or iPhone, do the regular exercise of uninstalling the applications you never use.

Rename

General

An essential method to see more clearly in your files is to give them proper names. There is nothing worse than a folder full of anarchically named files, such as:

- "Untitled1 (1).jpg",
- "Doc final version 2.jpg",
- "Anniv tata.jpg",
- "download.exe".

It is up to you and you alone to rename your files. The best practices in this matter are:

- Avoid names with less than 8 letters.
- Avoid names longer than 40 letters.
- Avoid using too many capital letters.
- Avoid generic names like "scanned file.jpg" or "letter.doc".

Folders
In terms of folders, there are names to ban: "Old PC", "Old hard drive", "Uncle's USB stick", "Old files", "Old". A lot of people use these kinds of names but it's too vague.

Documents
Choose names in three parts separated by dashes: "context - precision - date" or "context - date - precision".

For example, the file that contains your speech at a wedding may be called "Elsa and Luke's Wedding - Speech - June 2012.doc".

Your pay slips can be saved under names similar to "Pay slip - 2018.12 - Decathlon.pdf".

Dates
When it comes to dates, it is essential to name in order "year, month, day" and not the other way around, even if it is pronounced differently in spoken language. The sorting of the file will be all the better, as shown in these two screenshots.

01.02.2013.pptx
08.07.2018.pptx
09.09.2018.pptx
12.05.2012.pptx
12.10.2018.pptx
27.02.2018.pptx

2012.05.12.pptx
2013.02.01.pptx
2018.02.27.pptx
2018.07.08.pptx
2018.09.09.pptx
2018.10.12.pptx

Figure 7: Computers sort very badly the format day.month.year

Music

If the tags of your MP3 files are filled in, you should now avoid keeping files with abstruse names like "MichaelJacks.untITled.mp3", "Ilove.MP3" or "Untitled.mp3".

If your music file tags (attributes) are not up to date or if you don't know what they are, read the Organize chapter first.

Then simply use the MP3tag software to automatically rename all files in one of the following naming modes:

- Artist - Album - Title.mp3
- Artist - Title.mp3
- Artist - Year - Title.mp3

You'll get an elegant and orderly list of MP3 files.

It's more delicate for classical music. In general, the name of the artist of a classical piece is ignored or scorned: it is the composer who is important. It is then possible to opt for the following naming:

- Composer - Title.mp3

📖💻 *In the Tools chapter, a tutorial of MP3Tag is available.*

Photos

The storage of photographs is a work that can be very long and meticulous because it is the files that accumulate the most over a lifetime. According to the Business AM website, with the proliferation of phones, taking a picture has become such a mundane act that we photograph absolutely everything. As a result, the human race took 1,200 billion pictures in 2017, which is simply an all-time record. This is not surprising when you consider that an estimated 3 billion people own a smartphone if you consider the number of mobile subscriptions. And on average, people take 5 pictures a day.

For photographs, you can choose one of two approaches: either you date the folders and thematize the files or you do the opposite. Take a look at these two examples.

Figure 8: Two ways to name your photos

Renaming files from cameras or iPhones is particularly painful because these devices misname the photos. These are often incremental generic names such as IMG_5212.JPEG, IMG_5213.JPEG, IMG_5214.JPEG or P1000779.JPG, P1000780.JPG, P1000781.JPG.

At Android, especially Samsung, the situation is more concrete: photos are named with the year/month/day/hour/minute/second of their shooting.

For example: 20201026_132445.jpg

As for the music, there are attributes in the files of photographs. You can exploit these attributes to really detail your travel albums to the maximum. You can edit them in the file's properties.

Figure 9 : Properties of a photo

These attributes are then found in Windows Explorer.

Nom	Mots clés	Titre	Prise de vue	Auteurs
2017-02-10 - 012 - 2100003.jpg	New York; Mer; Statue; USA	Statue de la Liberté	10/02/2017 12:55	Juliette

The tool of choice for renaming a large number of files is Ant Renamer.

📖 💻 *In the Tools chapter, a tutorial of Ant Renamer is available.*

Videos

Films
It is best to avoid nesting too many folders together. Nesting all your movies in the movies folder is more than enough as long as you name the movies correctly with the following rule:

- Name of the movie (Year).mp4

For example:

| La Caravane De Feu (1967).mp4 | La Liste de Schindler (1993).mp4 | La Maison du Lac (1981).mp4 | La Mémoire dans la peau (2002).mp4 | La Momie (1999).mp4 |

| Les Oiseaux (1963).mp4 | L'Homme des Hautes Plaines (1973).mp4 | L'homme qui rétrécit (1957).mp4 | L'Impasse (1993).mp4 | Mamma Mia! (2008).mp4 |

Figure 10: Film storage

TV series
For series, the custom is to mix all the episodes in a folder dedicated to the series, taking care to name them well:

- Name of the series - Season - Episode.mp4
- Series name - sSSeEE.mp3
- Series name - **SSxEE**.mp4

SS = Season number. EE = Episode number in its season.

For example:

Friends -
01x01.mp4

Friends -
01x02.mp4

Friends -
01x03.mp4

Friends -
01x04.mp4

Friends -
01x16.mp4

Friends -
01x17.mp4

Friends -
01x18.mp4

Friends -
01x19.mp4

Figure 11: Storage of a TV series

Organize

The third rule to follow for a good computer hygiene is to organize your files. If you have deleted everything that is useless, then all that is left is to organize everything in folders.

There are four major files to fill out:

- Music,
- Videos,
- Pictures,
- Documents.

Music folder

The storage of music files resides in a protocol called "ID3". This computer protocol makes it possible to fill in all the usual criteria of a song in order to be able to classify them on demand. Indeed, it would be silly to use folders to store MP3s: how would you do it? By musical genre? By artist? By year? A music file contains too many attributes to use a single tree structure.

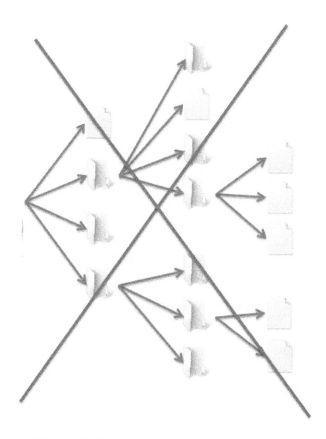

Figure 12: Don't store your music in subfolders

Under Windows, the attributes of music files can be viewed by going to the file's properties.

Figure 13: Attributes of a music file

The reduction of the musical mess thus consists in

1. Put all MP3s in the Music folder,

2. Fill in all MP3 attributes.

Focus on the most important attributes :

- Title,
- Album,
- Artist,
- Like,
- Year.

You will then be able to navigate easily thanks to software like MediaMonkey. This type of software takes into account the text attributes located in MP3 files in order to organize them by grouping titles that share common properties.

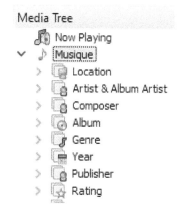

Figure 14: MediaMonkey offers a virtual music tree structure

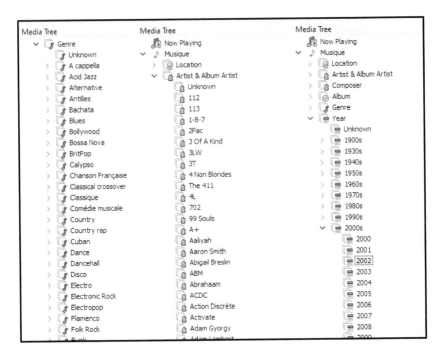

Figure 15: Multiple examples of browsing in MediaMonkey

📖 💻 *In the Tools chapter, a MediaMonkey tutorial is available.*

Once you've filled in all the attributes of your MP3s, you can embark on an extremely long but rewarding workshop: adding the illustrated covers to each song. It takes a lot of time, but can produce excellent results.

The tool of choice for adding a cover is MP3tag.

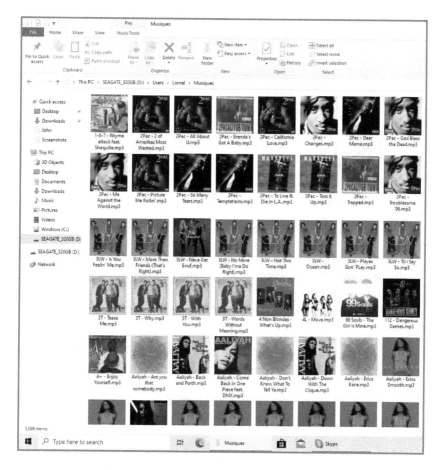

Figure 16: Windows displaying album covers

📖🖥 *In the Tools chapter, a tutorial of MP3TAG is available.*

Pictures folder

To organize your pictures, you should divide the "Pictures" folder into at least two subfolders: "Saved Pictures" and "Photos".

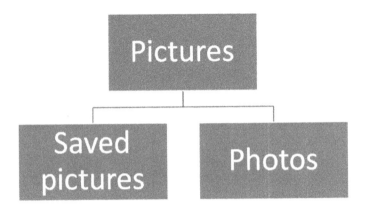

Figure 17: Two sub-folders of Pictures folder

The first one must contain the pictures that you have received or found on the Internet: jokes, anecdotal photos, city maps, advertising posters, various creations, invitation cards, logos, wallpapers, etc.

The second sub-folder is the one that will be dedicated to the storage of your photos. A good practice is to subdivide it itself into ten-year folders, which themselves contain annual folders.

In order to synchronize with a smartphone, a third folder must be provided to receive your photos.

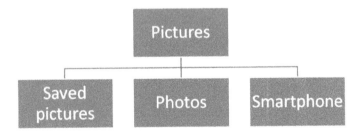

Figure 18: Third folder for the smartphone

Caution: do not leave the photos loose in a smartphone folder. Regularly, it is advisable to take a quiet hour to put away the photos taken with your smartphone: they should be distributed in the folders of the current year.

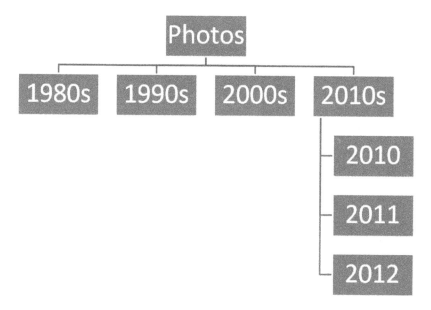

Figure 19: Temporal subdivision of the photos

Finally, each year must itself contain sub-folders. For this, there are two schools: those who arrange their photos by month and those who arrange them by event.

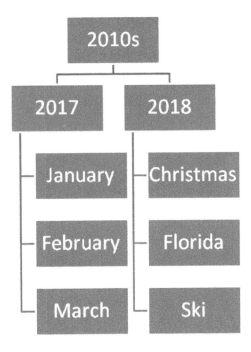

Figure 20: Subdivision by Theme or Month

Each year, plan a Miscellaneous file that will contain what you really can't categorize.

Videos folder

To organize your videos, you must first separate two subsets: commercial videos (films, TV series, documentaries, commercials, music videos, concerts, shows) and personal videos (children, weddings, travel, graduations).

The following tree structures can be recommended, for example.

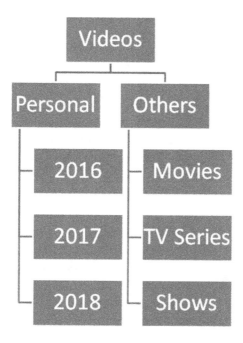

Figure 21: Example of the subdivision of the Videos folder

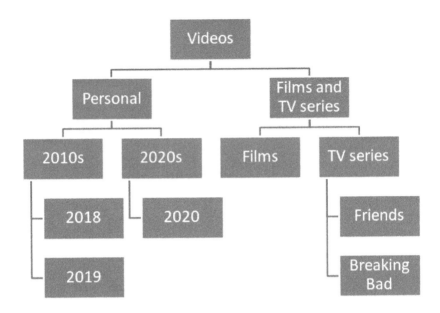

Figure 22: Example of video storage

Personal videos

In the case of home videos, there are several possible approaches. It depends on how many files you have.

There is the Decade/Year/Event method.

Here are examples of personal event file names: wedding, baptism, vacation, travel, children, birth, graduation, funeral, carnival, boom, judo competition, stay, walk, bar mitzvah, bachelor party, bachelorette party, new car, new house, Christmas, barbecue, farewell party, Ramadan, end of year show ...

Plan a miscellaneous folder, in every year, that will contain what you really can't categorize.

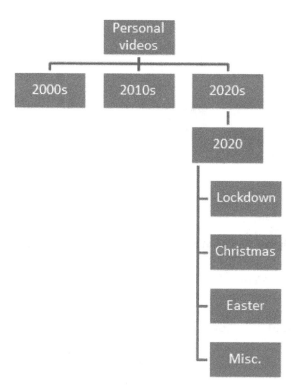

Figure 23: Example of a tree structure

If you don't have a lot of home videos, you can make do with Decade/Years.

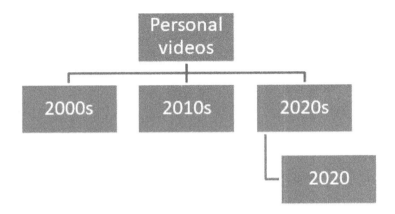

Figure 24: Another example of a video tree structure

Commercial videos
Sometimes, we may have to make a particular folder to group all the cartoons for example. It's easier to pick among the movies when a child asks for it.

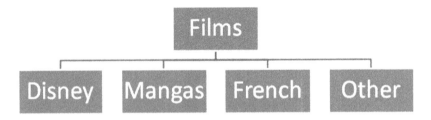

Figure 25: Subdivision of films by major categories

Documents folder

Anything that is not a video, picture or music is called a document. It can also be called office automation: Word, Excel, PDF, PowerPoint, Visio files, etc...

We can propose the following breakdown:

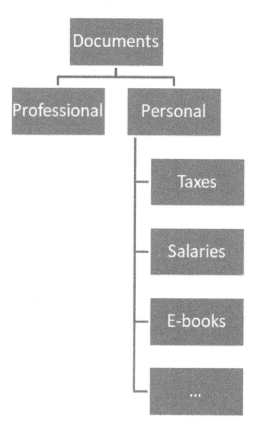

Figure 26: Example of document storage

It is traditionally the most heterogeneous file. Everyone has to find a way to organize it into different themes. For example: "taxes", "salaries", "health", "diplomas", "identity papers", "speeches", "e-books", "letters", "accounts", "CV", "EDF", "invoices", "bank", etc.

The way you store your office documents is very individual. The hardest thing is to keep this kind of file tidy from year to year.

Other folders in Windows

Beyond these four types of files, it is possible to have something else, such as:

- Game saves,
- Bitcoins,
- Source codes,
- Executables,
- 3D objects,
- Mailboxes,
- Password safes,
- Etc.

There are two ways to manage these "exotic" files. Either you include them in "Documents", or you create each time a root folder dedicated to them. Since Windows 10, for example, there is a "3D Objects" folder at the root of the user folders: it is used to store files to print 3D objects.

Objets 3D

Figure 27: 3D Objects folder in Windows

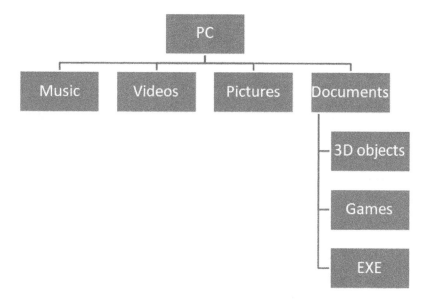

Figure 28: It is recommended to put everything that is not a picture, video or music in Documents

E-mails

There is a big tote bag that everyone has: the mailbox. We all have one or more of them and they contain hundreds or thousands of messages and attachments.

With the advent of Gmail, almost no one sorts or throws out their email, yet doing so is a task that contributes to the decline of digital mess. We can already do two things:

- Delete a few messages,
- Save some attachments.

Delete some messages

Regardless of the company that hosts your e-mails, there are three main areas of deletion to focus on:

1. Delete the oldest e-mails,
2. Delete the heaviest emails,
3. Delete the most useless e-mails, i.e. often spam and advertisements.

At Gmail, the king of consumer mailboxes, there is a very useful search tool for this.

It is located in a search box at the top of the https://mail.google.com/mail web page.

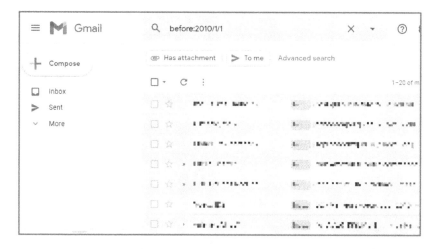

Figure 29: Example of a Gmail box

If you write "before:2010/1/1", Gmail will show you all of your emails prior to January [1,] 2010. Put any year in place of 2010.

If you write "larger:20M", Gmail will show you all your emails that exceed 20 megabytes. Put any size in place of 20 if you wish.

If you write "has:attachment", Gmail will only show you emails that contain an attachment.

These three searches can also be done by filling out a form.

Figure 30: Gmail search form

Finally, there is a method to track down and delete all advertising emails in Gmail. To do this, go to the Gmail settings and the "Labels" section.

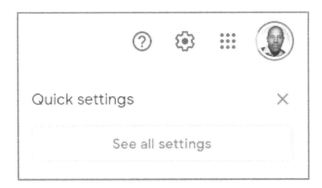

Figure 31: The parameters are in the gear wheel then "See all settings".

Then, click on "Display" the "Promotions". You will then obtain, if it was not already the case, a label "Promotions" in which Gmail deduces by artificial intelligence that some emails are advertisements or emails from commercial sources.

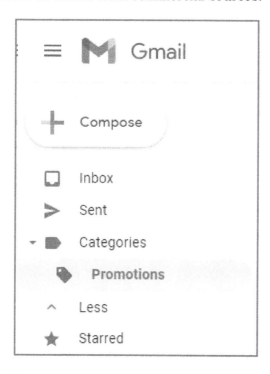

Figure 32: Promotions tend to be e-mails with little interest

Keep the attachments
Two problems arise when a user keeps attachments in his mailbox: on the one hand, they take up space and on the other hand, it is difficult to find them later. Let's take the example of a friend who sends you an important document that you asked him to scan. He names his file Scan0005.pdf and sends it to you in an e-mail with the subject line "Here as requested". When you open this email, you will understand what your friend is sending

you. However, if in 6 months or 6 weeks, you are looking for this attachment, you will have a hard time finding it because the name of the email and the name of the file are not precise enough.

So, the best thing to do is to save the attachment to a smartphone, computer or cloud.

Figure 33: Everything is misnamed in this e-mail

The e-mail box acts as a catch-all, but by carefully taking the attachments out of it, it will be easier to access later on.

External hard drives or external SSDs

External hard drives are durable, high-capacity storage media consisting of a magnetic disk enclosed in a case connected to a USB cord. They are devices that can hold a large amount of data for a fairly low price. SSDs are flash memories of the same use and tend to supplant hard disks. For the sake of abbreviation, in the remainder of this book, the term "external hard disk or SSD" will sometimes be reduced to "external hard disk".

Examples of November 2020 awards:

Capacity	Hard Disk Drive	SSD
500 GB	40 €	85 €
1 TB	50 €	150 €

If you are already using them, check their contents carefully: what you should not do is use an external hard disk or SSD to put files on them that you want to keep but that do not exist anywhere else. In case of theft, breakage, loss or failure of the external hard drive, these files will be lost for good.

We can classify in **three** categories, the cases of use of an external hard disk or SSD.

Transport
An external hard drive or SSD can be used as a means of transport to give someone a large file or folder that would take too long to send over the Internet.

Figure 34: Means of Transportation

Backup
An external hard disk or SSD can be synchronized with a computer to save its contents. It then contains the same data as the computer in question. On Windows, this backup can be done with the FreeFileSync software.

Figure 35: Backup

Extension
An external hard drive or SSD can be used as an additional storage place for a computer that is running out of disk space. It then complements the SSD or the internal hard drive of the computer. But in this case, another device must be provided to back up the whole thing (either a NAS or a cloud service).

Figure 36: Expanding Internal Storage

Other peripheral units

For most users, the digital mess inside their computer is compounded by a heap of files outside their computer.

Devices are a myriad of media that contain data but are not permanently connected to a network. They are "offline" objects. They include:

- USB flash drives,

- Cameras,
- Burned CDs,
- Memory cards.

The "offline zone" of your digital assets is the set of files that only exist in a single copy in the above-mentioned removable devices. These files are in your "blind spot": you cannot consult them without performing a manual action. This manual action is sometimes impossible. For example, if you forget at home a USB flash drive containing a very important presentation for one of your customers. You realize this once you get to the customer's office, but it is impossible to ask a USB flash drive to send itself over the internet.

Figure 37: The contents of USB sticks, CDs, etc. are sometimes out of reach of users: this is the offline zone.

A number of good practices need to be known. First of all, USB sticks, SD cards and cameras should be considered as transitory storage media.

The USB flash drive, in particular, is a means of transporting data and not a sustainable archiving device. This implies that it is better to regularly repatriate the files contained on these devices and then erase them. It does not make sense to keep a file on a USB stick as a single copy. On the one hand, the file is offline and therefore inaccessible unless a manual action is performed. On the other hand, if the USB stick is stolen, broken or lost, the file is unrecoverable. If you are given a file on a USB stick and you do not copy it to a computer, NAS or cloud, then the transport of that file is considered incomplete.

As soon as you have finished taking pictures with a camera, you should immediately connect it to a computer to back up your files. This is an obvious preventive measure against the loss of your digital photographs.

In the case of CDs and DVDs, a new concept appears: digitization. You may have noticed that there is not always a CD/DVD drive on recent computers. This is normal: this method of storage has become obsolete after only about twenty years of operation. Imagine these tens, hundreds of CDs and DVDs filled with music, photos, videos or documents from the 1990's/2000. Instead of letting them sink into oblivion, you have to take advantage of the latest optical drives available on the market to extract their contents. This act of digitization can allow you to rediscover some treasures, forgotten files that still have sentimental value for you.

Those who have time will be able to convert them one by one into immaterial files stored on a computer. The manual act of inserting the CDs or DVDs to play them will therefore never be necessary again. Remember that it is the medium that becomes obsolete, not the data that is written on it.

Lecteur DVD RW (E:)   Documents   Images   Musique   Vidéos

Figure 38: Digitization is the recovery of files from obsolete media

In this respect, the following chapter details how, technically, the digitization of optical media should be carried out.

Digitize

Digitization is the process of converting information into a digital (i.e. computer-readable) format. In this book, this concept will be assimilated to the "dematerialization", which is the activity of extracting data fixed on a physical medium in order to store it on a computer connected to the network.

This includes: photos printed on film, printed documents, MiniDisc, CDs, DVDs, audio cassettes, VHS, 8mm film, slides, camcorder tapes, vinyl, etc.

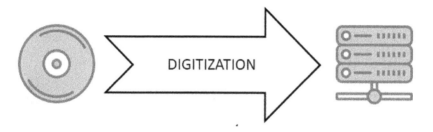

Figure 39: Digitization of a CD

Digitization consists in extracting content from the "offline zone".

This activity is made possible by the level of quality and performance achieved by computers and smartphones: high-fidelity sound and displays with excellent resolutions and colors. The "formerly manual" user experience of consulting photo albums or reading a CD is now reproducible with today's devices.

Figure 40: Older computers were not able to qualitatively reproduce music, movies, or photos. Nowadays, even smartphones have HD screens.

Digitization has the following advantages.

- **Sharing**. The file finally becomes diffusible to several people at the same time. Within the limits of copyright, it is better to share the contents of a CD or DVD than to keep it for yourself. It can be, for example, vacation photos from 1998, family videos or old e-books burned on CD.

- **Immediate availability**. No more need to make a research effort to go and consult a media. No more going to the basement, or taking a stepladder to look over a cabinet, or rummaging through a box full of unlabeled CDs. Nowadays, you expect to find everything without waiting. Digitization will allow you to achieve this result even with very old files.

- **Durability**. The risk of losing content is considerably reduced.

- **Anti-obsolescence**. Supports tend to become obsolete over the years. By digitizing their content, files can be taken through the decades without a hitch.

The disadvantages of digitization are as follows.

- This activity is costly in terms of working **time.** For example, each CD or DVD has to be put, one by one, into a drive. For most people, this is far too tedious.

- Digitization always requires special **equipment.** For CDs and DVDs, this is the optical drive as well as software, which is not necessarily free. It is potentially necessary to buy it because on recent computers, it is often missing.

- Finally, it's obvious: digitization requires abundant **storage** space.

To digitize an optical disk, four different cases must be distinguished.

- DVD video,
- Audio CDs,
- Blu-ray,
- Data CDs.

DVD video

As we all know, video DVDs are plastic wafers on which films, shows, documentaries or series are recorded. These supports, invented at the end of the 90s, have an anti-copying mechanism to prevent the general public from duplicating them. This mechanism based on cryptography did not resist for a long time and it is possible to convert a commercially available video DVD into a simple ".mp4" file.

The most powerful software in this area is WinX DVD Ripper Platinum. Sold at the price of 55 euros on the https://www.winxdvd.com/dvd-ripper-platinum/buy-fr.htm website, this software has a very simple user interface. It is important to note that neither this software nor its use is illegal. What is illegal is to distribute the obtained files. Legally, whoever owns the DVD has the right to keep his copy(s) for backup purposes. You cannot give a video file to a friend if you keep the original DVD.

📖💻 *In the Tools chapter, a tutorial of WinX DVD Ripper is provided.*

By converting all your DVDs to mp4 files, you don't have to increase your digital mess. Store them in a "Movies" or "TV Series" folder in the "Videos" folder of your computer or NAS for example. You will now have the chance to watch one of your old movies with just one click. In a few years when nobody will have a DVD player anymore, you will still be able to watch your movies like in the good old days.

This is the ambivalence of digitization: it mixes obsolescence and modernity. Once again, it is not the file that must become obsolete, but only the medium.

Aladdin (1992).mp4	Cendrillon (1950).mp4	Fantasia.mp4	La Belle et la Bête (1991).mp4	La Belle Et Le Clochard.mp4	La Fée Clochette.mp4
La Petite Sirène (1989).mp4	La Princesse et La Grenouille (2010).mp4	La Reine Des Neiges (2013).mp4	Le Retour de Jafar.mp4	Le Roi Lion.mp4	Les 101 dalmatiens (1961).mp4
Les Aristochats.mp4	Raiponce (2010).mp4	Vaiana (2016).mp4	Winnie l'Ourson (2011).mp4	Winnie L'Ourson Bonne Année.mp4	Winnie l'ourson et l'éfélant.mp4

Figure 41: Collection of DVDs that have become MP4 files

It is important to note that the resolution of DVD movies is 576 x 720 pixels, much less than HD or 4K. So, don't be surprised or disappointed.

Blu-ray

To extract movies from Blu-Ray discs, you can use the MakeMKV software available here: http://www.makemkv.com/.

It is a very easy to use software, free for 70 days. It generates MKV and not MP4 files.

Audio CD

Audio CDs were invented in 1982. They are not protected by any anti-copying mechanism because this aspect of copyright protection was not thought of in the 1980s.

To extract an audio CD, it is necessary to have an optical reader as well as an extraction software of which the most known is CDex. Then just put the CD in the player and launch an extraction that will generate one MP3 file per track.

After extracting all the tracks from all your audio CDs, your computer will have become the equivalent of a jukebox: one of those mythical devices that hold several albums of music.

📖 💻 *In the Tools chapter, a CDex tutorial is available.*

Data CD

Last category of optical disks: those containing files. These do not require a lot of work and do not require any specific software: just copy and paste their contents to your computer's hard drive. In the early 2000s, it was common to burn photos, MP3 music or DivX (pirated movies burned on CDs). This digitization session allows you to get your hands back on old memories.

Caution: do not digitize CDs containing software. Software is a computer program that becomes obsolete or even dangerous over the years. If you find software on an old, dusty CD, it is likely to contain software vulnerabilities that have since been fixed but have remained intact on the CD.

Once you have completed this digitization, you can say goodbye to all your optical media for good.

Paper

Digitization is also synonymous with the abandonment of paper. On a global scale, paper is losing ground:

- Books are replaced by e-books,
- Magazines are read on the shelf,
- Invoices are received in PDF format,
- Photos are rarely printed,
- Airline tickets have become QR codes,
- etc.

This work of digitization can be done at the level of private individuals thanks to an ordinary device: the document scanner.

Figure 42: A document scanner

With your scanner, you can, if you wish, transform into JPG or PDF a large quantity of documents, of which here are some examples:

- Pay stubs,
- Diplomas,
- Identity papers,
- Birth certificates,
- Medical prescriptions,
- etc.

These important administrative papers can be worth going through in digital format because sometimes it is easier to look for them in a computer than in a cabinet.

Have you ever thought about losing your passport in the middle of a foreign country? If you have a scanned version at your fingertips, it will be easier to prove your identity until you find a French embassy.

Sometimes, you are at the office and you take a few minutes to do some administrative work when suddenly you are asked for "proof of address" or "photocopy of spouse's identity card". Normally, you have to wait until you get home to look for these documents, but if they are already digitized, you can get them instantly.

Another category of documents that you can scan, and not the least, is all of your silver photographs printed on paper. Prior to the year 2000, most family photos existed only in paper form. Taking them to scan them one by one is a long job but it will only have to be done once.

If you don't feel brave enough, some companies offer this kind of service for a rate proportional to the number of photos.

Slides

It should be explained to younger readers of this book that a slide, often simply called a slide by apocope, is a piece of reversal film showing a single photograph and inserted into a plastic or cardboard frame. It is intended to be projected or viewed through transparency.

Figure 43: A slide was used to display a large photo on a white wall or canvas screen.

Figure 44: Showing slides required a projector

To convert slides, you will need to purchase a slide converter. This is a device that sells for about 90 € on the Internet. You will have to put the slides one by one into the scanner and it will produce in exchange, photo files to be stored in your computer.

Figure 45: Slide scanner

After converting your paper photos or slides into files, there will be no more holes in your photo folders.

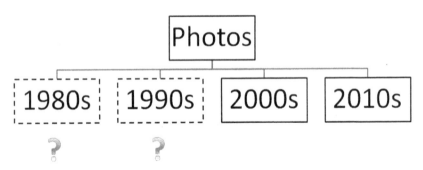

Figure 46: Most people do not have pre-2000 photos in their computer because they have not digitized old photos or slides of their family.

VHS

VHS is the official name for "video cassettes". They are the video equivalents of the silver photos: a support of memories of the years 80/90/2000.

The previous figure indicated "Most people do not have pre-2000 photos in their computer. Following this sentence, it can be said that most people do not have videos of their family prior to the year 2000.

Figure 47: A VHS cassette

In families with a camcorder, one of the members usually took care of filming the various family events. In those days, there were a multitude of video storage formats, but by and large, everyone managed to "dub" (i.e., transpose) the tape from the camcorder to a VHS cassette because that was the most common format for playing it on a VCR.

Then, like any technology, the VHS cassette became obsolete around 2004. The camcorder having been invented in 1983, we can approximately say that, in the families that have taken the trouble, there can be about twenty years of videos recorded on VHS.

Most people have abandoned these videos to their sad fate, in a cellar, a wardrobe or under a bed. Maybe they've even gone into the trash.

Figure 48: Videos by the author of this book, taken from VHS from 1988 to 1997

Yet it is frustrating to have part of the home videos as files and another part as old, unusable tapes! To solve this problem, we need to digitize VHS, i.e. transform each of these cassettes into MP4 video. Wouldn't it be great to see videos of you in the 90s again? Or maybe even see your parents' wedding video for the first time?

To perform this digitization, turn to Google and search for "VHS Transfers", "VHS Conversion", "Cassette digitization" and you will get a mass of results because this business is booming. Indeed, we, who have lived before and after the advent of IT, are the right generation to make this conversion. It's up to us to convert these files before they're forgotten or before any VCRs stop working.

Reading the title of this book, you thought you would only learn how to organize your files, but in fact, you now know that you have to create new files by doing some historical research. Explore your family's basements and closets in search of these precious artifacts and bring them to a video conversion lab as a matter of urgency.

Figure 49: Example of a video conversion lab website

Then, view, name and store these files carefully. When you do, feel free to share these files with your family, for example by offering them the videos on a USB flash drive, or by any other means.

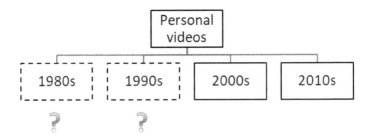

Figure 50: The digitization of VHS will finally allow you to have the videos of the 80s and 90s at your reach.

8mm or Super 8

Before camcorders, some families (generally rich) used to film their family events in a cinematic format on 8 mm film called Super 8. This format lasted from 1965 until the arrival of camcorders in the mid-1980s. Usually there is no sound.

As with VHS, you will need to call a lab for help to extract videos from 8mm film and convert them to mp4 files. This will allow you to add even older memories to your home video collection.

Figure 51: 8 mm personal camera

Super 8 films are immediately recognizable by their aged look, 4/3 ratio and outdated colors. They have a certain charm even without a soundtrack.

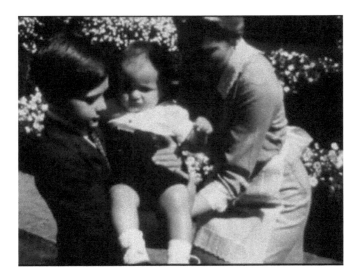

Figure 52: Excerpt imitating 8mm, from the film "The Game" - Universal Studios

Vinyls

Our tour of old media ends with the LP, still nicknamed vinyl.

This kind of disc is both old and current. Indeed, out of nostalgia, this support is in strong comeback since the end of the years 2010. Turntables that can play vinyl had almost disappeared from everyone's homes, but they are back in stores with extended features such as thinner designs and the ability to convert records to transportable digital formats such as MP3 or FLAC (a format with better quality than MP3).

Figure 53: a vinyl record

Figure 54: Turntable, released in 2019. It is USB and Bluetooth compatible

With this kind of turntables, it is now possible to buy vinyl records (or use the ones you already have at home) and then convert them yourself into an MP3 or FLAC computer file.

Arrange and name these files and enter their attributes as explained in the previous chapters.

The advantage of this method is that nostalgic music lovers will more easily get their hands back on songs they loved before. The disadvantage is that you have to admit that the digitization of vinyls is slow and tedious because you have to cut out each song and name it manually.

Centralize

Context and doctrine

Whereas twenty years ago, the only device containing files was the personal computer (PC or Mac), nowadays, dozens of devices play this role: camera, USB flash drive, box, smartphone, car radio, tablet, game consoles, and so on.

Figure 55: An individual typically owns more than one piece of computer equipment

Personal computers, smartphones and tablets are the "online zone" of your digital assets: they are devices connected to the Internet.

The multiplicity of devices quickly raised a problem: how to share files between all these distinct objects? How to make sure not to fragment one's digital heritage? It would be a shame to have his photos from 2002 to 2007 on a computer, his photos from 2008 to 2012 on a smartphone and those from 2013 to 2018 on a tablet.

The most common case is having your office files and old photos on your PC, MP3 files and recent photos on your smartphone and some videos on your tablet.

To put an end to this fragmentation, it is therefore necessary to centralize the files on an umpteenth device which will have to play the role of referent. By convention, this device should be considered as the owner of the main version of your files. Great communicator, this device will have to be able to restore or update your files at any time of the day or night while remaining connected to the others.

In our time, we can enact the following tidiness doctrine:

"Any user file must have an online accessible version".

Figure 56: "Every user file must have an online accessible version." This means that any file must be accessible without requiring manual action such as, for example, plugging in a USB flash drive or going to a specific device.

By "user file" it is necessary to understand file having a direct use by the users. That is to say, it excludes what are called "System" files, those that allow the operating system to work.

The consequences of this doctrine are as follows:

- If I have a photo in my smartphone and it is the only device in the world that contains this photo, I am in violation of the doctrine because it is not possible to view this photo from another device via a network. It is said that the file is offline. Nevertheless, I can still see this photo on my smartphone screen.

- If I have a file that is on a USB stick only, then I am in violation of the doctrine because I have to make a manual action to read the file: i.e. plug the USB stick into a computer.

The term "online" should be detailed. Wikipedia tells us that "a system (computer, network) and by extension its use or what it contains, is said to be **online** if it is connected to another network or system (by means of a communication "line").

Historically, the first way we used to put a file "online" was through the mailbox. Indeed, when you consult a file from your mailbox, you access a file online. Anywhere in the world, if you connect to the web interface of your mailbox, you will see your messages and the files they contain, also called attachments. It is therefore an archaic method of putting files online.

Figure 57: This e-mail contains an attachment. It is therefore online and accessible via Gmail.

Another method has been around for a long time to put files online: FTP. These are file servers accessible by an address, a port, a username and a password. But it is even more archaic and not very accessible to the general public.

Putting online means centralizing

Unlike previous generations, today's technology users are used to accessing everything, anywhere, anytime. Wifi, 4G, smartphones and other current technologies have made computing almost magical! To bring our personal files into this "magic", we need to centralize them, group them together, store them in a single place, in a single device that will be accessible 24 hours a day, 7 days a week, 365 days a year.

Whether he is in Mexico, Japan, in his living room or in his car, day or night, the user will be able to access his files in the same way.

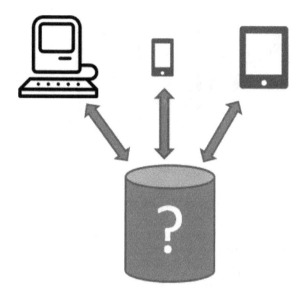

Figure 58: A device must federate the others

Only two devices exist to properly meet this need for centralization: the NAS and the cloud. They make up the "core zone" of your digital assets.

The NAS

A Network Attached Storage (NAS) is a computer server that is permanently on, connected to the local network and whose main purpose is to store or restore files.

This kind of device can be bought in shops for a minimum price of 159 euros.

Figure 59: Photo of a NAS

The NAS is a kind of computer without a screen, keyboard, mouse, webcam and speakers. Its main function is to be available to play or record files from other devices. Its storage capacity allows you to keep a large number of files at home.

If you're convinced of the benefits of NAS, you'll need to take a few steps to get there.

First, you will need to know how much storage capacity you need. For example, 1TB, 2TB or even 8TB. The storage capacity you choose should anticipate your future needs. If you're short on 1 TB of disk space today, choose 2 TB right away.

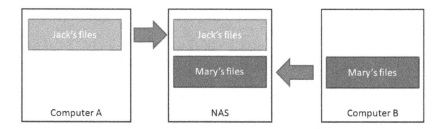

Figure 60: The NAS contains a copy of the entire family's files

You have to think about the fact that the NAS will be the only device that will contain the files of the whole family. If Jack has 1 Terabyte of files, and Mary has 1 Terabyte, Jack and Mary must at least purchase a 2 Terabyte NAS. It is even advisable to get a larger one in the future.

Next, compare NAS manufacturer brands. There are at least four of them that trust the market.

- Synology (the best known)
- Western Digital
- QNAP
- Asustor

Be careful to buy a NAS with included hard drives or you will have to buy them separately and then start a computer science job to insert the hard drives into it.

Figure 61: Some NAS are empty. Hard drives purchased separately must be inserted.

There are two categories of NAS: the cheapest models contain only one hard drive. They are less robust than those with two drives, so avoid them. Having two disks in a NAS is a guarantee of failure resistance: both hard disks contain the same files, which will allow the NAS to continue working even if one of the disks fails. This mechanism is called RAID.

Then the installation of NAS is a delicate subject. They are very simple devices in appearance ... except on the day they are installed. Since each model works differently, it is impossible in this book to dwell on the steps involved in installing a home NAS. But here are the overall steps:

1. Connect the NAS to its box or router with a commonly supplied **network** cable.
2. Connect the NAS to the wall **outlet.**
3. Follow the "First Steps" **manual** provided in the package.
4. **Create** user **accounts and folders.**

Once the NAS becomes the center of your IT infrastructure, you need to configure all your other devices to "turn" to it to exchange data with it. This data exchange can take two forms:

- Streaming playback,
- Synchronization.

Here is an example of a diagram that shows a NAS located at the center of an ecosystem of five devices. The PC and smartphone are in sync while the TV, stereo and tablet are streaming to the NAS. For the stereo and TV, there is usually little alternative because these are devices that have no storage memory.

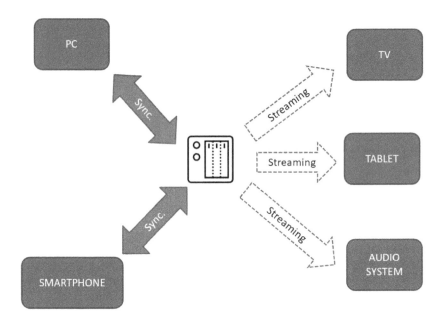

Figure 62: Diagram of a NAS and its ecosystem

Terminal mode / Streaming
Streaming, or streaming, consists of playing back content sent by a server (in this case, the NAS) without storing what is received. In practical terms, it means playing back files from the NAS with another device, such as a stereo, TV, or touch tablet. A device that performs this type of remote reading can be considered a "terminal". It does not have any files, but it can read files from the NAS.

For example, in one family, Juliette can watch a movie stored in the NAS, while in the next room, Emma listens to music stored in the same NAS. Finally, Marc browses vacation photos, also stored in the NAS.

Figure 63: The NAS as the center of multimedia entertainment

The advantages of streaming playback are:

- No use of terminal disk space,
- Certainty to read the latest version of the file,
- Changing devices is child's play: just buy a new item, log in and you can see all your files,
- In case of theft of the device, we know that no file will fall into the hands of the thief.

The disadvantages of streaming playback are:

- Out of use if there is no more network,
- Loss of quality if NAS and/or network are overloaded.

Could the PC, once a device overflowing with files, become a simple terminal like any other, devoid of files? From the year 2015, the traditional hard disk drive began to enter a phase of decline. Computer manufacturers are leaning more and more towards SSDs instead of hard disks because they are faster. On the other hand, these tend to contain smaller capacities. So, in 2017, it is as common to buy a computer with 2 TB of hard disk as it is to buy a computer with only 256 GB of SSD storage. The combined effects of this tiny storage (such as 256GB SSD) and the new uses of cloud and NAS are slowly pushing users into a so-called "terminal mode". The PC is reduced to a "reader" role that allows us to view or modify our files located remotely. For several years now, in companies, employees have been formally forbidden to write any file on their professional computer. Everything must be saved on the network.

Synchronized mode

Synchronization is something else entirely: it consists of ensuring perfect file replication between two devices, in this case the NAS and another connected object.

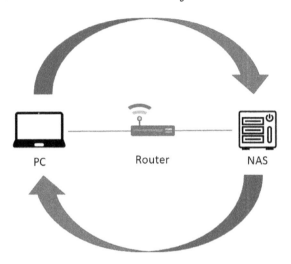

Figure 64: Simplified diagram of cyclic synchronization

Unlike the terminal, the synchronized device actually contains files and, several times a day, it takes care of contacting the NAS to synchronize with it, i.e., to pass on the files newly created, modified or deleted since the last synchronization. This is called "replication". It has files that are constantly updated with the NAS.

Figure 65: Most commonly used symbol to represent synchronization

There are several synchronization modes. The two most common are the so-called "mirror" synchronization and "bi-directional" synchronization. Mirrored, a B folder has instructions to look exactly like an A folder. This kind of replication therefore involves a template folder and a mirror folder. This mode is represented in this book by a unidirectional arrow. Conversely, the bi-directional mode allows each of the two folders A and B to influence the other.

The advantages of synchronization are:

- Files accessible even without a network ("offline"),
- The speed of file access does not depend on the load of the NAS or the network.

The disadvantages of synchronization are:

- Requires disk space on the replicated device,
- Does not guarantee that the file being read is the most recent.

Link between NAS and Smartphone
Now let's see how a smartphone can interact with a NAS. The following diagram gives an example of synchronization to be configured between smartphone and NAS.

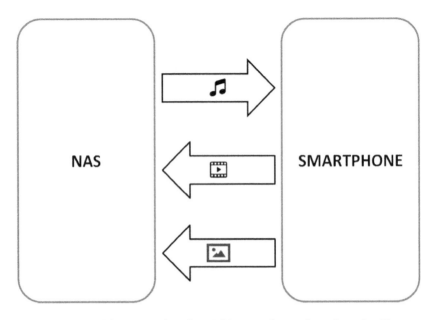

Figure 66: Example of NAS/Smartphone Synchronization

We can imagine a synchronization system in which the NAS automatically sends MP3 files to the smartphone so that the user always has the latest music at hand. On the other hand, the smartphone regularly sends its photos and videos to the NAS to put them online and save them.

In case of permanent loss of the smartphone, only the few photos and videos taken since the last synchronization will be lost. Hence the importance of opting for a synchronization mechanism that acts at regular intervals.

On Android, there are several synchronization applications. Let's take the very efficient "Syncme Wireless" as an example. This application is rather easy to configure, works on any Android device and allows you to establish a synchronization mechanism with a NAS. All you have to do is fill in the name of a folder in the smartphone, the name of a folder in the NAS and specify which one should be copied to which and the matter is settled.

📖 💻 *In the Tools chapter, a SyncMe Wireless tutorial is provided.*

For photos and videos, there are two ways to perform one-way synchronization. Either the backup is done by copying, or it is done by moving. In the first case, the photos and videos taken with the smartphone are copied to the NAS. In the second case, they are copied to the NAS and then immediately deleted from the smartphone. This second method is the one that respects the greatest need for privacy because the smartphone is regularly purged of its intimate files. Few people will opt for this method because smartphone users like to look at or show the pictures they have in their device, such as people who have children, those who are returning from trips or those who have just bought an apartment.

For a fixed PC (= desktop computer), its risk of theft or loss being rather low and its storage space rather large, one can embark on a full and bidirectional synchronization as shown in the following figure.

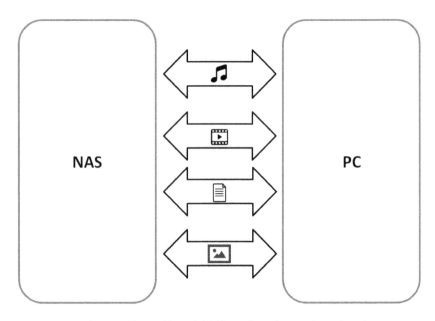

Figure 67: Full and bidirectional synchronization

Bidirectional synchronization is the process of replicating file changes in one direction or the other. The contents of the NAS and the PC are perfectly synchronized. This is a great precaution against file loss. If the NAS fails, the user keeps a perfect copy of his files in his PC. Conversely, if the PC dies, the NAS contains the files. Therefore, this file redundancy should not be considered a waste of storage space.

There is an excellent and free software to perform its synchronizations on Windows: FreeFileSync.

📖💻 *In the Tools chapter, you will find a tutorial explaining FreeFileSync*🖱️

The following table gives you an ideal configuration between "terminal mode" and "synchronization mode" for four types of devices. It presents a trade-off between the advantages and disadvantages of the two modes, depending on the type of device. For example, a desktop computer has a lot of storage space and has little risk of being stolen, so we can synchronize all our files on it. On the other hand, a tablet usually has little disk space, so we will only use it to read files remotely.

	Smartphone	Tablet	Laptop	Desktop
Documents	Terminal	Terminal	Synchro	Synchro
Music	Terminal	Terminal	Synchro	Synchro
Pictures	Synchro	Terminal	Synchro	Synchro
Videos	Terminal	Terminal	Terminal	Synchro

Sharing the NAS with your family
The NAS, as the central element of your installation, must be properly stored. The folders at the root of a NAS are called "Shares". Each family member must have a named share. Keep it simple: choose people's first names as the names of the shares.

Another share, usually called "Public" can be set up to store files that will appeal to the whole family. In Public, be sure to focus on files with no sentimental value and "general-public" content such as movies, TV shows, music videos, or music. To use a home analogy: the NAS is a family home, each named share is a bedroom, and the "Public" share is the equivalent of the living room.

Reducing digital mess also means segregating the files of each member of a family. Nowadays, devices are mainly individual: everyone has their own computer, smartphone, tablet. But the NAS is unique in the home. It must therefore be clearly configured so that no one encroaches on other people's data.

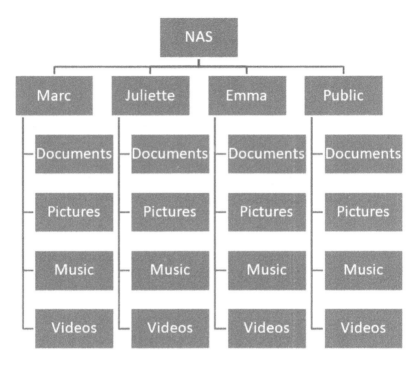

Figure 68: Separation of family members in the NAS

If Marc and Juliette accept that each one sees the other's files without allowing him to modify them, access rights must be configured. The same applies if they want to forbid their daughter, Emma, to see their files. Emma, who is secretive, doesn't want anyone to see her files.

	Marc's share	Juliette's share	Emma's share	Public
User Marc	Writing and reading	Reading only	No access	Writing and reading

User Juliette	Reading only	Writing and reading	No access	Writing and reading
User Emma	No access	No access	Writing and reading	Writing and reading

This configuration must be done in the NAS Management Console.

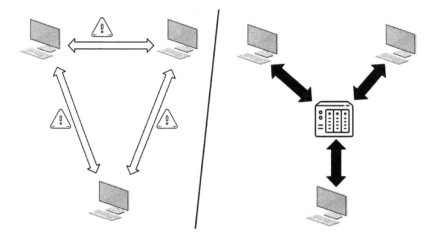

Figure 69: The puzzle of file sharing between computers is over when you have a NAS

This file sharing capability of the NAS is a strong factor in reducing digital mess. Indeed, it is no longer necessary to duplicate files on all devices in the family. Marc's vacation photos are in his folder on the NAS, so Juliette will be able to look at them without having to have a copy. As long as the NAS is turned on, and Marc allows his files to be viewed, Juliette will be able to look at her photos.

The NAS mimicking VOD platforms
What if you became your own VOD (video on demand) host? Plex
is a client-server multimedia management software that allows
you to access movies, series, music and photos on the server no
matter where the client is located, if he has an Internet
connection. It is divided into 2 parts:

- The Plex server, which can be installed on the NAS. It
  contains and organizes the files and will manage the
  client connections.
- The Plex client that receives the content from the server
  through a web browser (via the website) or an application
  for mobiles, connected TVs, PCs, ...

The visual presentation of Plex is surprisingly close to those of
famous VOD platforms. But this time, all the movies are yours!
The visual interface is much more beautiful than that of
Windows. Compare.

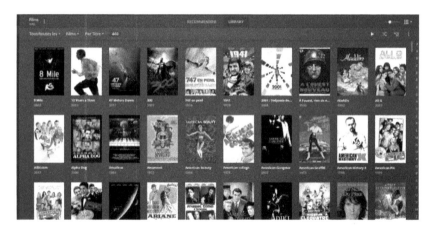

**Figure 70: Plex generates its own movie covers by listing
users' movies on the NAS**

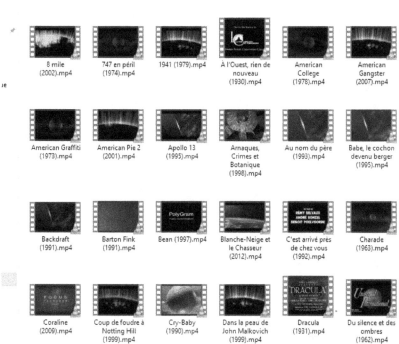

Figure 71: Here is the same collection of movies but on Windows

Warning, Plex is not available or installed in all NAS brands. At Synology, it's a free optional package to install. It's quite simple to install.

Then the navigation between the movies is a real pleasure, worthy of the Netflix interface. The movies come in particular from the ones you digitized in the previous chapter.

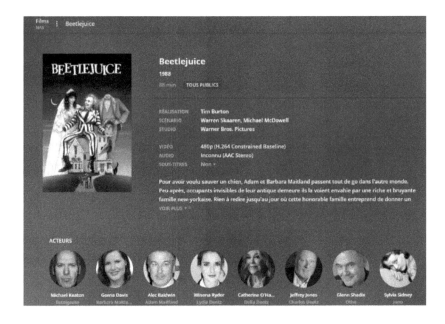

Figure 72: Self-generated display of Beetlejuice movie details in Plex: synopsis, sleeve, year of release, actors, etc.

Figure 73: Plex also manages TV series

Warning: Plex does not encourage illegal downloading. It's just a file binder. As seen in the digitization chapter, you may very well have files from DVD or Blu-Ray purchased legally and by you.

The NAS even outside the home
To compete with the Cloud concept, NAS manufacturers all offer the possibility to view and even modify the content of NAS even outside the home through secure remote access mechanisms.

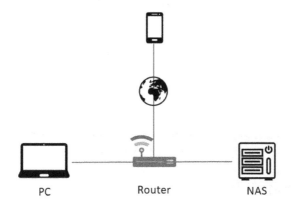

PC   Router   NAS

Figure 74: A NAS is often accessible even outside the home, for example with a smartphone

The manufacturer of the NAS provides applications (Android and iOS) and a website to access all the files on the NAS. Whether you are in front of the NAS or 18,000 kilometers away from home, it makes no difference: your files follow you in your pocket. The centralization of the files therefore has as a side effect, their ubiquity. This ease of consulting your files remotely from your home should encourage you not to put too many files in your smartphone or laptop.

This data roaming is an essential feature of the new generation NAS because it allows the user to be nomadic without overloading his smartphone with files. You can look at pictures of your children on a business trip or continue to watch a movie in a waiting room that you didn't have time to finish the day before.

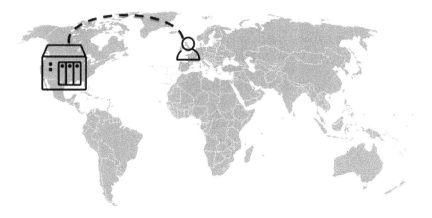

Figure 75: Most NASs allow you to view or modify your files anywhere in the world.

The Cloud

Definition
The cloud is the generic name given to online file storage services. It is the big competitor of the NAS. It has advantages and disadvantages.

The concept of cloud is a neologism that the general public has been hearing about since the beginning of 2010. This technology consists of hosting files in the shared servers of external companies. This storage located "elsewhere" is represented by a cloud to reflect the ease and ubiquity of the service.

Figure 76: Commercial representation of the cloud

With the concept of the cloud, the general public is voluntarily left in the dark. Users do not know and do not need to know where and how their files are stored. The invisibility of the cloud's hardware infrastructure supports the concept of the cloud being full of data (rather than rain) and ubiquitous around us.

So, to demystify the thing, here is, in exclusivity, the brick and mortar representation of a cloud, on the following figure.

Figure 77: Exterior of a data center

The cloud is a service provided to users through one or more data centers (data centers), a kind of computer factory that contains corridors and hallways of permanently lit computers.

Figure 78: Interior of a data center

The distance that separates a user from his data is totally unknown to him, but it is very likely that it is on the same continent as him, with another permanent copy to the data center on another continent. This data redundancy ensures that the user will not lose access to his data even in the event of a failure.

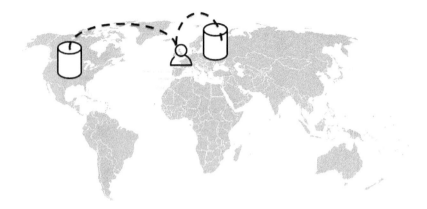

Figure 79: Geographic redundancy

Even if a disaster strikes the data center in the United States, consumer files will still be available thanks to the data center in Poland, for example.

Another redundancy exists at the level of the servers themselves: RAID. This storage technique ensures that even when one hard disk fails, one or more others continue to function while it is being replaced. This technology is found in some NASs.

Figure 80: In data center servers, each file is stored on several hard disks.

Advantages/disadvantages

Can cloud storage services be trusted? The answer is yes, but we must remain wary on the following three points.

Unlike the NAS, the user is no longer in full control of his files. If the U.S. government wants to consult them, they can do so. And if the hosting provider closes your account or goes bankrupt, the service stops.

In case of any Internet failure, your files are no longer available. This will be the case if your box breaks down for example or if you are in an area not covered by 4G or Wifi.

If for any reason your account is terminated, you lose all access to your data.

Another disadvantage of the cloud, unlike NAS, speeds are slow if you don't have the fiber. It is necessarily faster to transfer a file on an internal network than on an external network if you only have ADSL. With fiber, the transfer times of Cloud or NAS are equivalent, especially with Google Drive.

Conversely, the advantages of cloud services are numerous. First of all, the cloud saves you the fatigue of buying and installing a NAS in your home. This is a very big advantage for people who are not comfortable with computing. All you have to do is subscribe. Nothing to install, nothing to connect.

The second undeniable advantage is the physical security of your data. Stored in large, redundant warehouses, your files are safe from burglary, fire, power outages, theft, and water damage, while the NAS hosted at home is highly vulnerable to all five of these disasters.

The third advantage is the durability of the service. You're pretty sure that the service will last for years, whereas a normal NAS will tend to fail one day.

The fourth advantage of the cloud is its level of adaptation to needs. To expand your storage space, you simply subscribe to the higher offering and it's done in a minute, while to expand the space of a NAS, you have to replace or unscrew it and add or replace a hard drive.

But overall, the result is the same with a NAS or cloud service: your files are centralized. There are two modes of operation: streaming or synchronization.

As with the NAS, online file storage services can be synchronized or just streamed. The following diagram shows the most common usage.

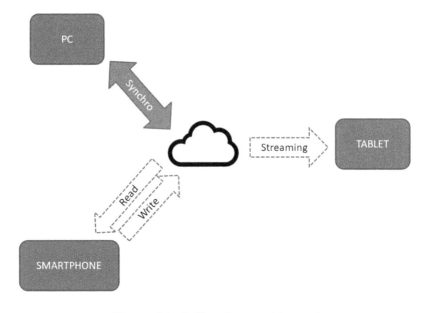

Figure 81: Online Storage Ecosystem

By installing a simple application on your smartphone, you can be assured that all your photos will be automatically saved in the cloud wherever you are. Conversely, you can view all the photos in the cloud with the same application.

Figure 82: Saving and consulting photos/videos

For office automation, it's the same. The user can write Word documents or fill in Excel sheets from a smartphone or tablet.

Figure 83: It is possible to use a smartphone + a cloud service for office automation, just like on a PC

Depending on its constraints, it is then possible to work in "offline" or "online" mode, i.e. to leave the file in replication on the smartphone or only to modify it remotely in the cloud without occupying the smartphone's disk space.

On a computer, it is similar. There are also the two operating modes: if you want to work on the file remotely without dropping it on the computer, you just need to access the cloud service with a simple web browser. Conversely, if you prefer the replication mode, then you need to install a small software program that will ensure synchronization between the computer and the cloud.

Rates and operation

To subscribe to a cloud storage service, it is necessary to make a small comparative study of the current offer. Some providers offer free subscriptions for small amounts of storage.

The first step is to evaluate the amount of GB or TB (Gigabytes or Terabytes) needed to store your digital heritage.

Many cloud storage offerings are free or included in packages you already own. For example, your Internet service provider may offer you free cloud storage.

Here is a study of storage prices in November 2020 for some known cloud services.

Google Drive

Storage	15 GB	100 GB	200 GB	2 TB
Price	Free	1,99 €/month	2,99 €/month	9,99 €/month

One Drive

Storage	5 GB	100 GB	1 TB	6 TB
Price	Free	2 €/month	69 €/year	99 €/year
			+ Office Pack	+ Office Pack

Dropbox

Storage	2 TB	3 TB	5 TB	Unlimited
Price	9,99 €/month	16,58 €/month	10 €/ user/ month	15 €/ user/ month

Amazon Drive

Storage	5 GB	100 GB	1 TB	
Price	Free	1,99 €/month	9,99 €/month	

As depicted in advertisements, the cloud is very easy to use, without any configuration.

Choose the right capacity according to your needs.

Once you have subscribed to a cloud hosting service, you get storage space from your hosting provider. This storage space is accessible through a URL address.

Most hosting providers have opted for a similar ergonomic interface: service logo on the top left, tree structure on the left and file area on the right.

For example, https://drive.google.com/drive/my-drive for Google Drive:

Figure 84: "Empty" cloud at Google Drive (8.4 GB out of 15 are already occupied by Gmail emails)

Another example is https://onedrive.live.com for Microsoft OneDrive:

Figure 85: Empty cloud at Microsoft OneDrive

Third example, at Amazon Drive, with the URL https://www.amazon.fr/clouddrive/.

Figure 86: Empty Cloud at Amazon Drive

You now need to install the small module to synchronize your files. It is a program that will run regularly on your PC or Mac in order to pass on in real time all your file creations, modifications and deletions to the cloud.

To get this synchronizer, you shouldn't have any difficulty: Microsoft OneDrive's synchronizer already exists on all Windows 8 or 10 computers worldwide.

For others, look for the "Get Applications" or "Download Drive for PC" links, usually at the bottom left of web pages.

For example, at Google Drive, you get this page: https://www.google.com/drive/download/

Figure 87: Page to download the module from Google Drive

Click on "Download" (from left) to get the following installation file:

installbackupand
sync.exe

Figure 88: Google Drive Synchronizer for PCs

Double-click on it to install it and then follow the installation questionnaire:

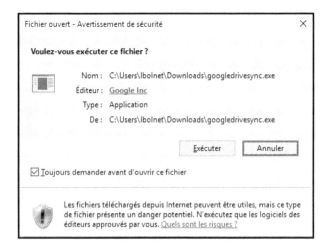

Figure 89: Windows Security Warning

At some point, you will be asked for your Google Account login and password in order to authenticate your connection to the cloud.

Figure 90: Authentication Page

Once logged in, Google Drive tells you that a "Google Drive" folder has been created on your computer. From now on it is this folder that will provide the synchronization gateway between your computer and the cloud. Everything in this folder will also be in the cloud and vice versa.

Figure 91: The first time you put files and folders in the Google Drive folder, a copy of each will immediately go to the Google cloud.

Now, feel free* to drag and drop your four folders - Music, Documents, Videos, and Pictures - to the Google Drive folder (or OneDrive, or Dropbox, whatever).

*Warning: it is up to you to know if you have subscribed to sufficient space for all your files. If you exceed the space allocated to you in the cloud, you risk either a malfunction or a price increase. Be sure to measure the size of your files before you subscribe.

Figure 92: You must move and not copy

All that remains is to wait.

When a file or folder is on its way to the cloud, you see a small blue circle on its icon:

Figure 93: Folder being synchronized

On the other hand, if the icon has a small green check mark then it means that the synchronization is complete and therefore the file or folder is perfectly identical in the computer and in the cloud.

Ready Folder

Figure 94: Folder completely synchronized

The synchronization time depends on the speed of your internet connection and the size of the files you have. It can therefore take a minute, an hour, a day, a week or more...

It is strongly discouraged to have an ADSL connection to use a cloud hosting. It is too slow. Prefer fiber.

The speed of the cloud is also to be taken into account. Compare the speeds of the following services (test carried out by uploading and downloading a 54.5 Mb file on December 22, 2018 with an upload connection of 5 Mbps and a download connection of 100 Mbps).

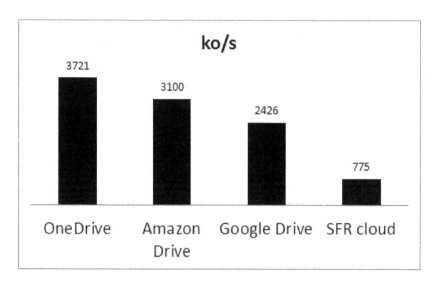

Figure 95: Upstream test (2017)

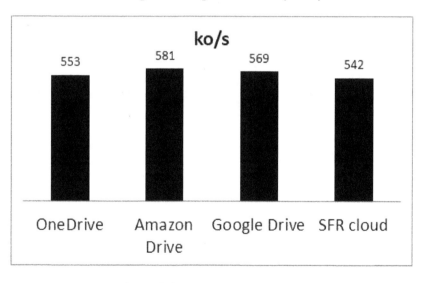

Figure 96: Downstream Test (2017)

Once the synchronization is complete, you'll find that your files have all arrived in the cloud.

Figure 97: View of your folders in Google Drive, with a PC

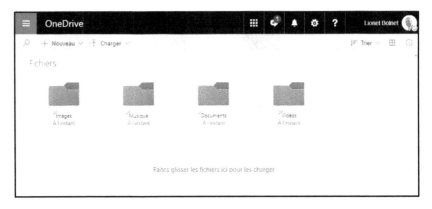

Figure 98: View of your folders at OneDrive with a PC

All you have to do is use your files as you did before. Anything that happens to them will be reflected in the cloud.

Action	Repercussion in the cloud
Creating a file	Creating the file
Renaming a file	Renaming the file
Moving a file	Moving the file
Editing a file	Modification + versioning
Deleting a file	Trashing

On Google Drive, you can even back up multiple computers. For example, if you have a work computer and a home computer, your files will be stored separately in this group:

Figure 99: Computer separator in Google Drive

Versioning
Thanks to versioning, you will be able to find the old versions of each file. This is handy if you have accidentally changed a sentence in a Word document and can't remember what was marked before.

To do this, go to the web page of your hosting service and right-click on the file and enter the "Manage versions" menu:

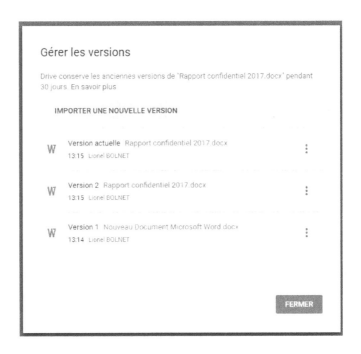

Figure 100: Version management in Google Drive

Smartphones
For smartphones, it's the same: start by downloading the Android or iOS application from the cloud service of your choice.

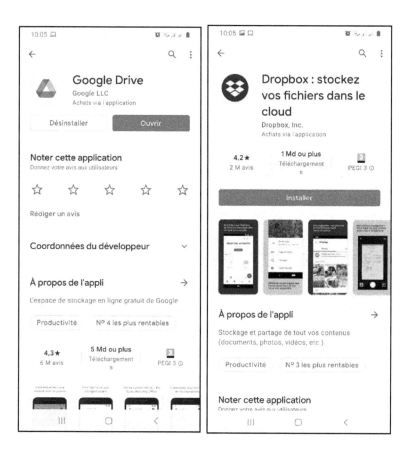

Figure 101: Screenshots of the Google Play store

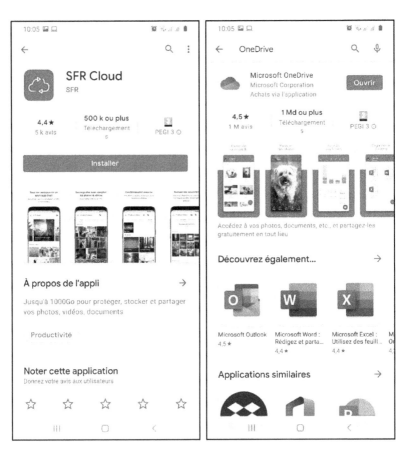

Figure 102: Screenshots of the Google Play store

Then launch the application and log in with your credentials or create an account if this is your first use of the service.

The manipulations are rather intuitive.

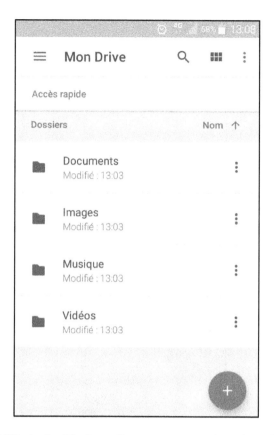

Figure 103: Android view of your space at Google Drive with Android

To ask the application to permanently back up your files, the steps are usually quite simple.

Figure 104: Capture of the Backup menu of the Google Drive app, under Android

Zero PC trend

Cloud services such as Google Drive or OneDrive are unsuitable for large video files such as movies and commercial series. On the one hand because of the long transfer times and on the other hand because cloud services reserve the right to delete video files if they believe they infringe copyright.

A cloud user will tend to opt for three distinct services:

- **A VOD or SVOD service** to watch movies and series.
- A legal **music** streaming **platform service.**
- **A storage service** in the cloud for your photos and documents.

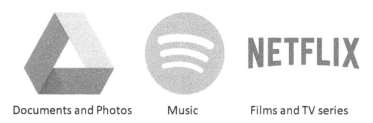

| Documents and Photos | Music | Films and TV series |

Figure 105: Three examples of services in the cloud for different uses

With these turnkey services, there is even a trend to make the good old personal computer disappear and with it, the digital mess.

- The stereo or Bluetooth speaker is directly connected to Spotify or Deezer (or other streaming music platform).
- The television is directly connected to Netflix or Amazon Prime (or other VOD or SVOD platform).
- The tablet is used to modify or read documents stored in the cloud.
- The smartphone is used to coordinate everything or to look at his photos stored in the cloud.

Such a user simply finds himself without a computer at home! This "zero PC" trend appeals especially to younger people. They are consumers rather than computer users. They don't want to have to manage devices and files.

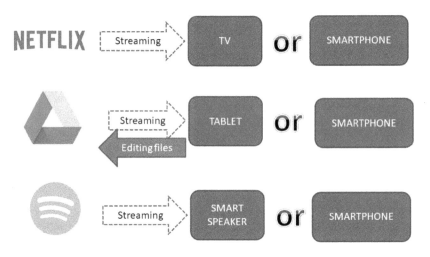

Figure 106: Example of an ecosystem centered on clouds

The issue of confidentiality

It is crucial to emphasize that an "online" file does not necessarily mean "available to the whole world". It is obvious that every person has the right to have personal and secret files.

The discipline that ensures that a file is only accessible to those who have the right to access it is cybersecurity: a set of technical and technological measures that prevent access to a file by strangers.

Whether it's the NAS or the Cloud, there are theoretically enough security measures in place to prevent 99.9% of the time someone from accessing your files without your permission. Zero risk does not exist, but it is similar to the risk of a burglary of your home. If having all your files at hand is not important to you, then don't put them online. But then again, you take other risks in life that are much greater, like driving a car, or not having a 4-point lock on your front door.

To reinforce the confidentiality of your files before putting them on a Cloud, you can also opt for an encryption mechanism, i.e. a device that "encrypts" each file with a password.

For the NAS, it is different, you can encrypt the entire NAS with an encryption key. By doing so, you further reduce the already low risk of your files being intercepted.

In a simpler way, make sure you take responsibility for your own cyber security by following the security recommendations of your NAS or Cloud service provider. For example, choose long and complicated passwords, enable two-factor authentication (the login mode that sends you an SMS to verify your password).

Similarity between centralization and backup

All these notions of file centralization are very similar to the concept of backup. On the whole, one must keep in mind that a file saved on a single medium runs the risk of being lost. You must have at least two copies of each file.

Backup

Backing up files is not, strictly speaking, an activity that helps reduce digital mess, but its implementation is in line with the activities presented in the previous chapters. If you don't back up your files, all the work done in the previous steps may go up in smoke.

The volatility of files is a psychological brake for many people. We have all experienced the loss of a file or even an entire computer due to a bug, virus, false manipulation, hard drive corruption or a fatal laptop crash. These moments have hurt us because we have lost a 200-page report, a folder of photos or a handful of e-mails. And since then we no longer trust these devices. We mourn their solidity. We sulk about them for fear that they will hurt us in the same way.

However, it is possible to regain computer confidence with a simple habit: regular backups! This activity, which consists of copying a file to another medium in order to use it if the original is lost, is an unavoidable reflex in companies, but this reflex escapes the general public completely. If you don't want to have to rewrite a 200-page report, then the solution is simple: save it regularly, that is, not just at the end of its writing.

For smartphones, it's the same. The majority of people do not back up the content of their smartphone. It's quite edifying: people spend a fortune on smartphones (sometimes 800, 900, 1000 euros) but make no effort to keep the content (photos or videos). They have a strong attachment for the device but no attachment for the photos or videos they take. This is totally illogical. If you ask anyone on the street, "please show me the oldest personal photo you have", you are very likely to get the answer "I don't have the photos from my previous smartphones because they broke with hundreds of files inside".

Be aware that even if you change your smartphone every 12 months, this does not mean that you should systematically throw away the files they contain. You should always keep your digital assets.

The copy cycle

Whether it's smartphones or PCs, you need to overcome media obsolescence, i.e. to maintain the integrity of your digital heritage as you purchase equipment, thanks to the copy cycle: you need to regularly back up your files by copying them from one medium to another. This method will prevent you from losing them.

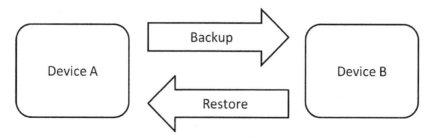

Figure 107: If device A regularly sends a copy of its files to device B, the risk of losing its files is reduced. Whether A or B fails, the data will always be in the other one.

Note that the spatial distance of the devices is fundamental in terms of backup: device A and device B are each a backup of the other provided they are far apart. If, for example, you have in your backpack a laptop and an external hard drive that contains a backup of the laptop, you are still in danger of loss because if your bag is stolen in the subway, you have lost everything. To avoid this, you should keep device B in a completely different place than device A, usually at home.

Support The Guardian
Available for everyone, funded by readers

Contribute →   Subscribe →

😀 Sign in

The Guardian

News | Opinion | Sport | Culture | Lifestyle | ☰

Coronavirus World UK Environment Science Global development Football   More

Technology

Having your laptop stolen is traumatic. Here's what I learned

According to research, a laptop is stolen every 53 seconds - but how prepared are you for what comes next?

Figure 108: Newspaper article about a student who loses months of work when his computer is stolen

The doctrine of safeguarding is:

"Any user file must have another identical copy stored on another device".

In certain aspects, the concept of centralization, previously described in this book, is similar to that of backup. The difference is the notion of an "online" file.

The backup also gives the opportunity to perform a versioning. This consists of keeping a different copy of the same file for each backup cycle. This is used to find a file as it was several minutes ago and thus to restore a false manipulation.

Figure 109: Versioning allows you to go back in time to find the old state of a file.

For example, this book was backed up dozens of times during its writing (on average every 10 minutes).

📄 Vaincre le désordre numérique - v2.docx 2020-11-17 014501.docx	17/11/2020 01:33
📄 Vaincre le désordre numérique - v2.docx 2020-11-17 013501.docx	17/11/2020 01:22
📄 Vaincre le désordre numérique - v2.docx 2020-11-17 012501.docx	17/11/2020 01:14
📄 Vaincre le désordre numérique - v2.docx 2020-11-17 011501.docx	17/11/2020 01:01
📄 Vaincre le désordre numérique - v2.docx 2020-11-17 010501.docx	17/11/2020 00:54
📄 Vaincre le désordre numérique - v2.docx 2020-11-17 005501.docx	17/11/2020 00:44
📄 Vaincre le désordre numérique - v2.docx 2020-11-17 004501.docx	17/11/2020 00:34
📄 Vaincre le désordre numérique - v2.docx 2020-11-17 003501.docx	17/11/2020 00:24
📄 Vaincre le désordre numérique - v2.docx 2020-11-17 002501.docx	17/11/2020 00:08
📄 Vaincre le désordre numérique - v2.docx 2020-11-17 001501.docx	17/11/2020 00:02
📄 Vaincre le désordre numérique - v2.docx 2020-11-17 000501.docx	16/11/2020 23:54
📄 Vaincre le désordre numérique - v2.docx 2020-11-16 235501.docx	16/11/2020 23:41
📄 Vaincre le désordre numérique - v2.docx 2020-11-16 234501.docx	16/11/2020 23:27
📄 Vaincre le désordre numérique - v2.docx 2020-11-16 233501.docx	16/11/2020 23:24
📄 Vaincre le désordre numérique - v2.docx 2020-11-16 232501.docx	16/11/2020 20:50
📄 Vaincre le désordre numérique - v2.docx 2020-11-16 205501.docx	16/11/2020 20:44
📄 Vaincre le désordre numérique - v2.docx 2020-11-16 204501.docx	16/11/2020 19:06
📄 Vaincre le désordre numérique - v2.docx 2020-11-16 191501.docx	16/11/2020 19:02
📄 Vaincre le désordre numérique - v2.docx 2020-11-16 190501.docx	16/11/2020 18:38
📄 Vaincre le désordre numérique - v2.docx 2020-11-16 184501.docx	16/11/2020 18:27
📄 Vaincre le désordre numérique - v2.docx 2020-11-16 183501.docx	16/11/2020 18:24
📄 Vaincre le désordre numérique - v2.docx 2020-11-16 182501.docx	16/11/2020 18:12
📄 Vaincre le désordre numérique - v2.docx 2020-11-16 181501.docx	16/11/2020 18:02
📄 Vaincre le désordre numérique - v2.docx 2020-11-16 180501.docx	16/11/2020 17:50
📄 Vaincre le désordre numérique - v2.docx 2020-11-16 175502.docx	16/11/2020 17:45
📄 Vaincre le désordre numérique - v2.docx 2020-11-16 174501.docx	16/11/2020 17:35
📄 Vaincre le désordre numérique - v2.docx 2020-11-16 173501.docx	30/01/2019 00:01

Figure 110: Successive versions of this book

Let's review the backup modes of five everyday devices.

Smartphone backup

Backup of smartphones became more widespread when they began to be entrusted with intimate information such as photos and videos.

There are four main methods for backing up photos and video from a smartphone. The first is simply by plugging the smartphone into a computer's USB port and then sending its content to the computer.

To Windows (Android procedure)
With Android, no specific software is required. But you need to know the Android tree structure.

Connect the smartphone with a USB cord and unlock its screen. You should see it appear in Windows:

Figure 111: In "This PC", the device appears. The icon in the form of a walkman is not very representative of a smartphone.

Double-click on the icon to see its storage space(s).

Figure 112: Two volumes, one for the SD card and one for the phone's internal memory.

For Android devices that have a removable memory card, there are two storage volumes. You have to know where to look for your files.

Photos and videos taken with the "Camera" app can be in:

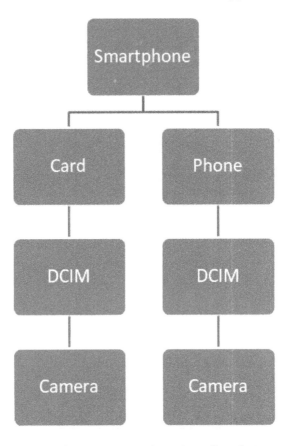

Figure 113: Primary storage locations for photos and videos

But note that there are pictures in other folders, for example, WhatsApp.

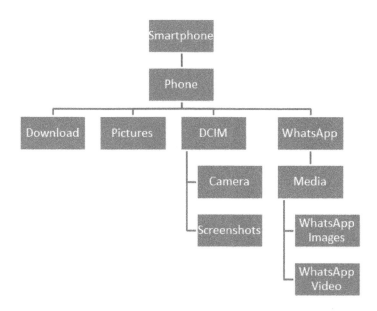

Figure 114: Other photo and video locations on Android

Then you can simply drag and drop files from your smartphone to your computer, in Windows.

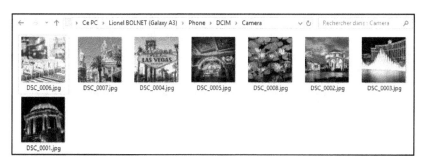

Figure 115: Content of a smartphone on Android seen from Windows

To Windows (iOs procedure)

At iOS, for photos and videos, no specific software is required. But you need to know the iOS tree structure.

Connect the smartphone with a USB cord and unlock its screen. You should see this appear in Windows:

Apple iPhone

Figure 116: In "This PC", the iPhone or iPad appears. The icon is not very representative.

Double-click on the icon to see its storage space.

Figure 117: At iOS, storage space is called Internal Storage

Double-click to enter the space to view the photo and video folders. Unlike Android, there are fewer:

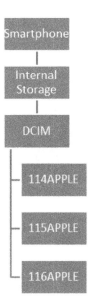

Figure 118: Photos and videos are in folders with names ending in APPLE

Then you can simply drag and drop files from your smartphone to your computer, in Windows.

> Ce PC > Apple iPhone > Internal Storage > DCIM > 114APPLE

IMG_4487.JPG   IMG_4482.JPG   IMG_4484.JPG   IMG_4481.JPG   IMG_4478.JPG

IMG_4486.JPG   IMG_4483.JPG   IMG_4485.JPG   IMG_4480.JPG   IMG_4476.JPG

IMG_4475.JPG

Figure 119: Content of a smartphone under iOS seen from Windows

To the cloud

The second method of backing up a smartphone is to install a cloud sync application such as OneDrive, Google Drive or many others. This concept has already been discussed in the Centralize chapter.

To a NAS

The third method is to install a NAS synchronization application such as the SyncMe Wireless application. Be careful, with SyncMe Wireless, you must be in the same network as the NAS so it is not possible to back up your device outside your home, in theory.

Fortunately, the NAS vendor offers a proprietary solution, for example Synology offers the DS File app, and Western Digital offers the My Cloud Home app. With these apps, you can back up your photos and videos even when you are away from home. This is a perfect mimicry of the Cloud apps.

📖 🖥 *In the Tools chapter, a SyncMe Wireless tutorial is provided.*

Figure 120: Capturing My Cloud Home in the Play Store

Figure 121: Capture of the DS FILE app in the Play Store

To a USB flash drive for smartphones

Finally, for a few years now, there has been a way to back up a smartphone without a computer, without a NAS and without a cloud: the USB OTG (On-the-go). This is a feature that is unfortunately not yet available on all devices. You must have a very recent model to benefit from it: the USB port of your smartphone can then accept to exchange files with USB flash drives.

Figure 122: USB flash drive for smartphone

By plugging a USB flash drive into a smartphone, the principle is to be able to easily retrieve its content and keep it in a safe place. To buy a USB flash drive compatible with smartphones, a small format verification exercise is required. Indeed, nowadays, there are three types of connections for smartphones: USB micro B, USB-C and the Lightning port of iPhones.

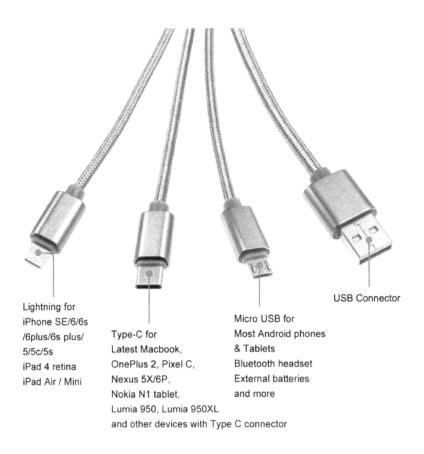

Lightning for
iPhone SE/6/6s
/6plus/6s plus/
5/5c/5s
iPad 4 retina
iPad Air / Mini

Type-C for
Latest Macbook,
OnePlus 2, Pixel C,
Nexus 5X/6P,
Nokia N1 tablet,
Lumia 950, Lumia 950XL
and other devices with Type C connector

Micro USB for
Most Android phones
& Tablets
Bluetooth headset
External batteries
and more

USB Connector

Figure 123: Three types of connection for smartphone + the normal USB port

So, choose carefully the right USB flash drive for your device, or opt for the four-headed models outright!

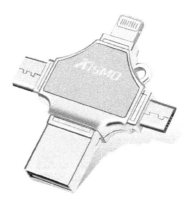

Figure 124: USB flash drive compatible with everything!

It is also possible to put an adapter between a "normal" USB flash drive and your smartphone:

Figure 125: Adapters normal USB to Smartphone

Then use the file browser app on your smartphone to copy and paste files to the USB flash drive. At Samsung, for example, the app is called "My Files".

Figure 126: On Samsung, use the My Files app to copy files from to the smartphone USB flash drive

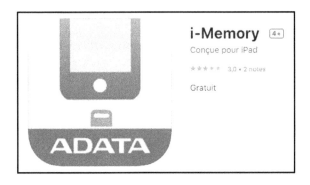

Figure 127: In iOS, the i-Memory app allows you to copy files to a Lightning USB flash drive.

Remember that you no longer need a computer to copy files from a smartphone to a USB flash drive. This is good news for the "Smartphone" generation, which is gradually moving away from traditional computers.

Tablet backup

The backup modes of a tablet are identical to those of a smartphone:

- Cloud,
- NAS,
- OTG USB flash drive
- PC.

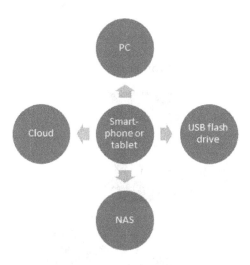

Figure 128: Make sure to back up your tablet and smartphone files somehow

Personal computer backup

There are only three truly reliable methods of backing up files on a personal computer.

The first involves a cloud service as mentioned in the previous chapter.

The second involves synchronization with a NAS. This is also discussed in the previous chapter.

The third method of backing up a computer is simply the external hard drive or SSD. With the help of synchronization software, the external hard drive can succeed in getting exactly the same files as the computer. In the Tools chapter, you will find a tutorial to learn how to use FreeFileSync. This software evaluates the differences between two devices to copy only what has changed since the last backup.

It is also possible to set up a recurring backup system as long as the external drive is left connected at all times. This is especially valid for desktop computers.

Figure 129: It looks like a NAS but it is just an external hard drive connected 24 hours a day, via USB, to a PC.

By convention, here is the file structure that should be created in an external hard disk or SSD:

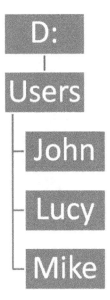

Figure 130: Usually, on the external hard disk, you have to create a Users folder and in it one folder per person. This is a usage convention.

Then, the external hard drive or SSD should be stored in a safe place or left connected at home. But you should avoid leaving the house with it, to avoid its loss or theft.

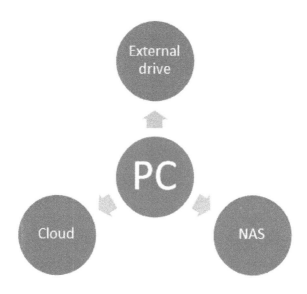

Figure 131: Make sure to back up your PC files in some way

Camera or flash memory backup

It is obvious that a camera needs to be backed up. There are about three ways.

The first, and most well-known, is to remove the memory card from the camera and then slide it into a computer. This method requires a computer with a memory card reading slot, which is very common. After that, just copy and paste the files with the computer's operating system.

The second way is the pure and simple connection of the camera to a computer via a USB cable. Afterwards you just have to copy and paste the files with the computer's operating system.

In the methods described above, the common point is that you must be near a computer to conduct the backup. This is constraining and risky because, if you wait, for example, until the end of a long trip to save your photos, you run the risk of losing them before the return (theft of the camera, breakage…). Fortunately, manufacturers have reacted. We are starting to see in stores, wireless backup hard drives, intended for photographers on a trip. The Western Digital SSD My Passport Wireless, for example, is an external SSD that has its own battery. It allows you to save your photos even in the wilderness. Its price is rather high: about 300 euros.

Figure 132: The Western Digital My Passport is the hard drive of the photo reporter.

This kind of device retrieves photos either by USB cable, by directly inserting an SD card or by WiFi signal. The photographer thus finds himself with two storage media for his photos. Back home, he will have to dump his photos into a computer, a NAS or a cloud.

Figure 133: Make sure to back up your camera contents

NAS backup

The NAS is a backup medium provided that the files stored inside of it exist on another medium. If your NAS contains files that do not exist elsewhere, then it has no backup skill. There are various methods to back up a NAS.

Figure 134: Synology NAS Backup Configuration Screen

With an external hard drive (local USB)
The simplest method is to connect the NAS to an external hard drive with a USB cable and then schedule a full copy of its contents to the external drive once a day. On the back of the NAS enclosure, there are always one or more USB ports. These can be used to exfiltrate the data from the NAS to an external backup hard drive. If the NAS fails permanently, the small external hard drive attached to it has a good chance to save your data. However, this method is powerless against fire, power outages, and any form of disaster that would impact the NAS.

Those who have a basement away from their home, can also make monthly backups of their NAS and keep the external drive in a safe place in their basement, away from thieves (unless there is theft in the basement) and fire.

To benefit from a backup to a media that is truly remote from the home that hosts the NAS, you need to consider the methods offered by the NAS vendor.

With another NAS

Most vendors offer to export the data from the NAS to another NAS of the same brand located elsewhere in the world. For example, if a family has a primary and a secondary residence, it is ideal to install two NAS, one in each home, and then make the primary residence's NAS copy itself every night to the secondary residence's NAS. This is called "NAS to NAS" backup. You still need to have the financial means to own two homes, two Internet subscriptions and two NAS!

Figure 135: Illustration of backing up a NAS with another NAS

With a cloud

Another method proposed by NAS vendors is to backup data to an online storage service. In this case, the proximity and velocity of the NAS is combined with the weather resistance of the cloud. However, beware of the expense that this configuration implies: the monthly cost of the cloud.

Synology Company offers a NAS Cloud offering called "Synology Cloud²". Another company named ElephantDrive is the specialist of the genre. It offers to back up your NAS remotely for $10 per month.

146

These services are called "hybrid solutions" because they combine the benefits of NAS and the cloud.

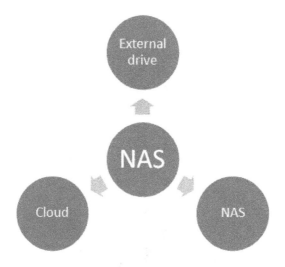

Figure 136: A NAS can be backed up to another NAS, to the cloud or simply to an external hard drive

Remember that if your NAS only contains copies of files from other devices, there is obviously no point in backing it up.

Cloud backup?

You cannot, strictly speaking, "back up the cloud". It's not up to you to do so. It is the company that offers you the service that makes backups of the cloud (for example Google, Microsoft or Dropbox).

On the other hand, it is strongly advised to keep a copy of the files you have entrusted to your cloud host. Why should you keep a copy? It is preferable to have an updated version of all the files you have in a cloud to avoid the following eventualities:

- Voluntary or accidental **deletion of** your files by the host,
- **Network outage** at home, preventing you from accessing the cloud,
- **Termination of** your Cloud subscription,
- **Bankruptcy of the** hosting provider, resulting in a sudden shutdown of the service,
- Sudden **price change** that forces you to pay to view your files in the Cloud.

This precaution of being able to access your files without the Cloud is called reversibility.

Figure 137: Whatever the device, keep a recent copy of your Cloud files: external hard drive, smartphone, PC, USB flash drive, NAS, ...

Warm and cold backup

The files that you view and edit year-round are stored primarily on your computer: they are the originals of your digital heritage. They "live": they are constantly being modified, deleted and added. They can therefore be considered "hot".

If you use an online backup solution, i.e. available at any time, via the computer network to which your computer is connected, you can set up a fairly high backup update frequency (once a day, once an hour or even in real time). This backup, which closely follows variations in the original files, can be described as "warm". Warm files are, within a few minutes or hours, identical replicas of "hot" files.

On the other hand, if you use an offline backup solution, i.e. not connected to your computer network, this backup can be described as "cold".

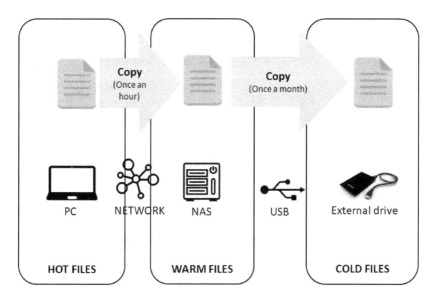

Figure 138: Double-safeguard: lukewarm and cold

The main advantage of cold backup is that it cannot be infected by a virus since it is not connected to the network. But there is another advantage: if you make a serious mistake, the warm backup may be impacted a few minutes later but not the cold backup. It bears its name of cold: the media is not electrically connected except at the time of the backups.

For example, one can plan a warm backup every hour and a cold backup every month. This way all your files will exist in triplicate. This is more prudent.

Synthesis

To save a file is to duplicate it in a second medium. For each type of device, there are solutions more suitable than others.

Smartphones, tablets, computers, USB flash drives, memory cards, cameras, Cloud, NAS, external hard drives are some of the digital devices of our time. Thanks to various wired and wireless technologies, it is easy to copy files from one to another. So, don't hesitate to own duplicates of all your files.

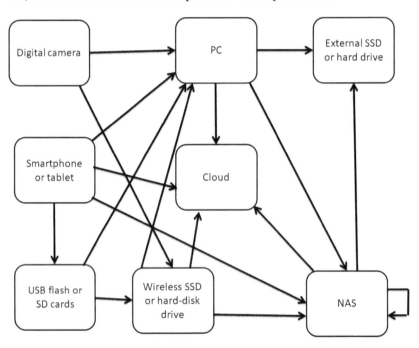

Figure 139: Each arrow shows the ideal devices for saving another one

Trivia

March 31 is World Backup Day every year. It's a day invented to raise awareness about backing up files. A dedicated website reminds us that 30% of people have never made a backup in their life and that 113 smartphones are lost or stolen every minute in the world!

Figure 140http://www.worldbackupday.com

Password management

Digital mess is not just about files and applications. Another form of digital mountain has been falling on our heads for twenty years: passwords! Every website asks us to memorize one.

How do I memorize my passwords?
Is it safe to write them on a piece of paper?
Is it safe to write them in an Excel file?

What not to do

Of course, passwords should not be written on a piece of paper, whether at work or at home. In the event of a burglary, the thief could connect to your bank and make a transfer, for example.

It is also not necessary to have an Excel file containing your passwords, otherwise in case of theft of the computer, a person will immediately know how to connect to your bank accounts, PayPal, Facebook account, taxes, insurance …

My
passwords.xlsx

Figure 141: What not to do

The first solution to save your passwords in a secure way is obvious but becomes difficult nowadays: memorize all your passwords in your head.

Figure 142: We are overwhelmed by passwords

It is necessary to have a **different password** for each company, because in case of data theft at company X, your password will necessarily be tried by hackers at all other known companies! If your PayPal password is the same as your password on Hippopotamus.fr then you make, in advance, a very nice gift to the data thief who will attack the Hippopotamus servers.

KeePass

Second solution: the password safe. It is an encrypted file that opens only if you know your password. Inside you can freely write all your other passwords.

Figure 143: The password vault allows only one password to be remembered

The most famous of these tools is KeePass. It can be downloaded from https://keepass.fr/.

After installing this software on your computer, launch it and go to "File" then "New" to create your first password database.

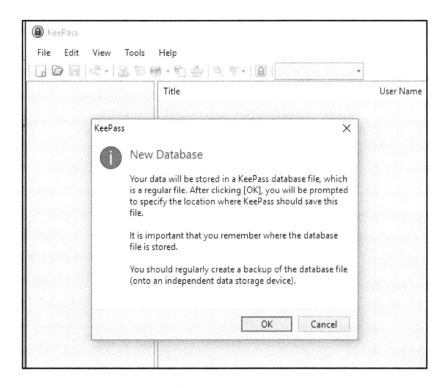

Figure 144: Basic Password Creation

Choose a name for your password database, then choose the password that will lock it. Be careful: no one will be able to help you remember it. Never forget it.

Save this file.

Figure 145: Choosing the password to lock the base station

KeePass will then offer you to print a backup sheet, i.e. a sheet on which your password will be printed. Do not do this.

This is where your password database is created. Start filling it in by clicking on the button .

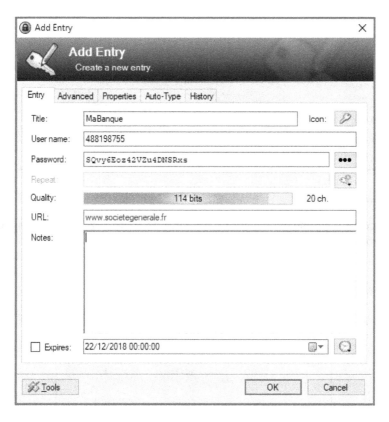

Figure 146: Fill in all the information you have

Don't forget to regularly register your safe with the ⊟.

You can, at any time, consult the list of your accounts:

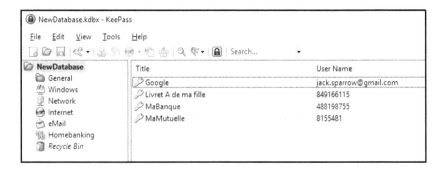

Figure 147: List of passwords

To copy a password without looking at it, just right-click on it, like this:

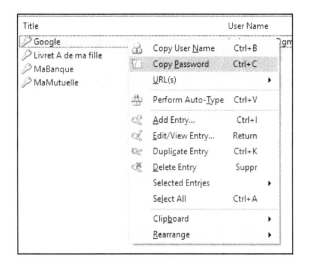

Figure 148: Discreet password copy

To see the password, double-click on the corresponding line and click on the " ... " button.

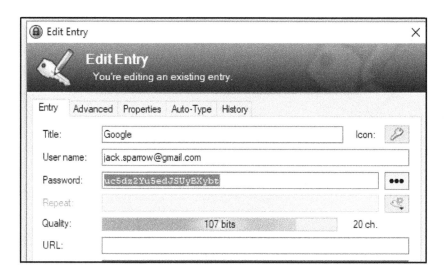

Figure 149: The password can be visible

If you close the KeePass, nobody can read your passwords anymore. The file is absolutely unreadable in Notepad.

Figure 150: The KDBX file generated by KeePass is unreadable if you do not know your password.

Figure 151: Dialog box to open the KDBX file

To some extent, this file is both valuable and widely available. Feel free to treat it as a normal file: take it with you to your smartphone or to the office. If your smartphone is stolen, the thief is unlikely to be able to read its contents.

Figure 152: KeePassDroid on Android

Cette app est uniquement disponible dans l'App Store pour les apparei

MiniKeePass 4+
Flush Software, LLC

★★★★ 3,9, 82 notes

Gratuit

Figure 153: MiniKeePass for iOS

Combine the power of SyncMe Wireless with the security of KeePassDroid, for example, to get an always up-to-date password safe from your NAS on your smartphone.

You can also send your KeePass safe from your PC to your smartphone via e-mail or USB cable.

No more worries about "What can my password be on this site? " Draw your smartphone, launch the KeePassDroid or MiniKeePass application, enter your unique password and pick the one you are looking for.

If your smartphone is equipped with a fingerprint sensor, you can even open your KeePass safe without entering the password!

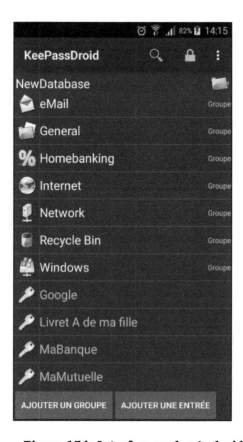

Figure 154: Interface under Android

Google Passwords

Those who use Chrome on PCs or smartphones may be surprised to learn that many of their passwords are kept by Google! Take a look at this site:

https://passwords.google.com/

Sign in with your Google credentials.

Figure 155: Google login screen

And you'll see how carefully Chrome has stored all your passwords on Google's servers.

Don't be shocked: Google saves your passwords in their secure cloud thanks to your Chrome entries. If this mechanism scares you, you can disable it in the Chrome settings and erase all passwords in Google Passwords.

Figure 156: List of your passwords at Google

To view them, click on the eye icon.

Figure 157: Example of a disclosed password

Tools

In the previous chapters, several tools running on PCs or smartphones were mentioned. This chapter will review them.

All these pieces of software are for Android or Windows.

MP3tag

https://www.mp3tag.de/en/

It is a program that allows you to enrich the attributes of MP3 music files. Much better than Windows Explorer, it allows you to view and modify the properties of mp3 files. One of its interesting functions is the renaming tool that allows you to name an mp3 file based on its attributes "performer name" and "title".

To do this, launch the application, drop music files into it, then go to the "Converter" menu and then "Tag -> File name".

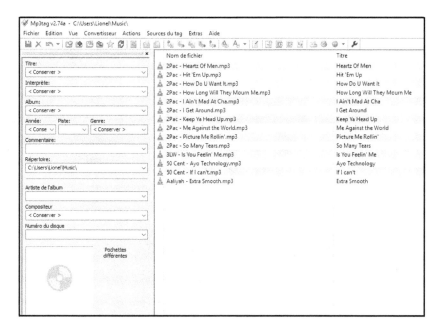

Figure 158: MP3tag's general screen

Make sure that the format is %artist% - %title% and click OK.

Figure 159: File renaming dialog box

MP4tag is also handy for filling in the attributes of mp3 files including their album artwork. This is done through the left part of the software.

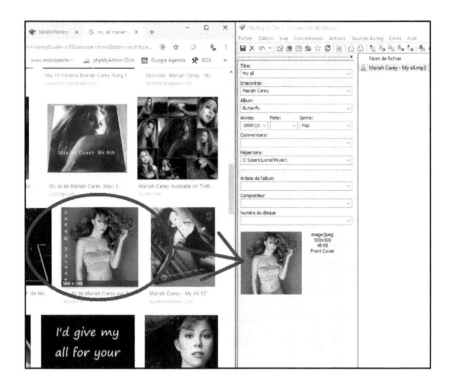

Figure 160: Dragging an Album Art to a MP3 song

To choose a cover, simply search for the album name on Google, go to the "Google images" results and then drag the picture of your choice to the small MP3tag frame.

DupeGuru

https://dupeguru.voltaicideas.net/

This software allows you to duplicate files: it scans one or more folders on your computer and compares their contents to indicate which ones exist in addition to one copy. Then it proposes to delete them.

Figure 161: The first step is to indicate the file to be audited.

Click on the "+" button to add one or more folders to browse. After clicking the "Scan" button, the list of duplicate files appears.

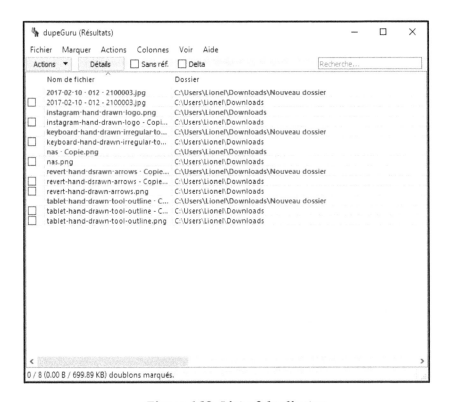

Figure 162: List of duplicates

Then it is up to you to decide whether or not to delete them. DupeGuru will then delete all copies except 1 for each file so that they are all unique.

FreeFileSync

https://freefilesync.org/

It is a free software that is used to synchronize files from two folders. The fame of FreeFileSync lies in its reliability and ease of use.

170

Be very careful when configuring this tool: think carefully about the direction in which the synchronization is going to be done and choose well the mode of deletion repertories.

On the official FreeFileSync website, download the executable file FreeFileSync_x.x_Windows_Setup.exe and then perform the following steps in order to set up the synchronization of a computer running Windows.

Create a SYNCHRO folder on your PC, for example, in C:/.

Install the FreeFileSync_x. x_Windows_Setup.exe file.

Create a versioning folder on the NAS. The "versioning" folder is the folder where all old versions of a file or files that have been deleted from your computer will be stored. It is like a kind of "Trash" folder. It is best to create it with the MS-DOS command "mkdir" and give it a name starting with a "dot". There should be one versioning folder per shared folder.

For example:

```
■ Invite de commandes
Microsoft Windows [version 10.0.10586]
(c) 2015 Microsoft Corporation. Tous droits réservés.

C:\Users\Lionel>mkdir "\\WDMYCLOUDMIRROR\lionel\.Corbeille"
```

Figure 163: Versioning folder

Thus, you get a hidden folder named ".Trash" or ".Corbeille" (in french).

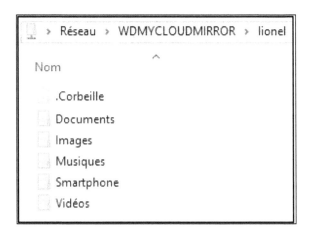

Figure 164: View from Windows Explorer

If the MS-DOS command scares you, you can create the "Trash" folder without the dot, by the usual method, but then the folder will not be hidden.

Start the FreeFileSync program. Specify the four pairs of folders to be synchronized. (If needed, create manually in the NAS, the folders for Pictures, Documents, Videos, Music). For example:

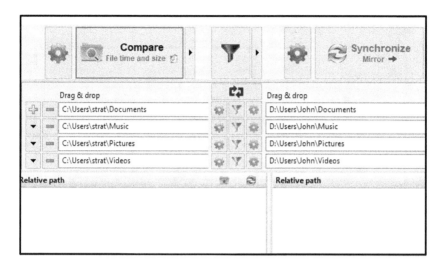

Figure 165: The 4 synchronization pairs

Then click on the blue gear to continue the configuration.

In the "Comparison" tab, remain in "File time and size" mode.

Figure 166: Comparison configuration

In the "Synchronization" tab, choose "Two-way" for bi-directional synchronization or "Mirror" for one-way synchronization. Choose a timestamp versioning mechanism and ignore errors.

Specify the previously created version storage folder: ".Trash".

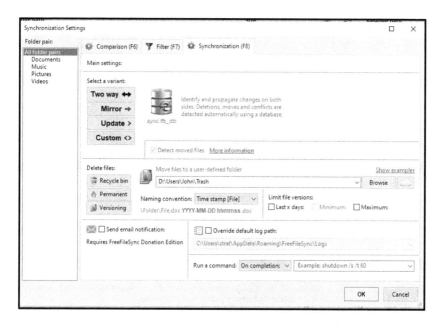

Figure 167: Synchronization Configuration: choose "Two-way", "Versioning" with naming convention "Time stamp FILE"

Then save the configuration file of your synchronization configuration as a:

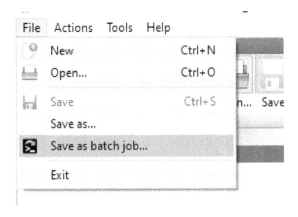

Figure 168: File menu. Save as batch job.

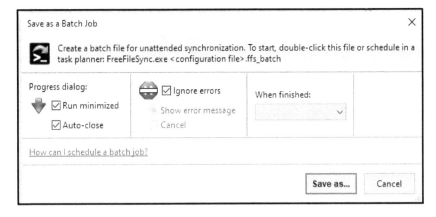

Figure 169: Save as Batch windows

Check the three boxes: "Run in minimized window", "Auto close", "Ignore errors".

And save it in the previously created C:\SYNCHRO folder.

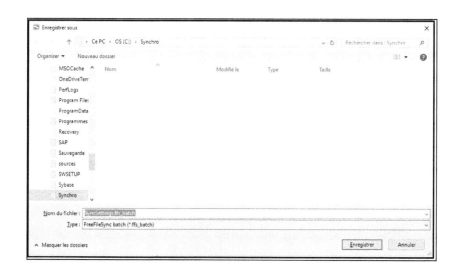

Figure 170: Save the configuration

All that's left to do is to create a task that will start the synchronization every 30 minutes (or every one hour). Start the

Windows "Task Scheduler" by writing "Tasks" in the Windows Start menu.

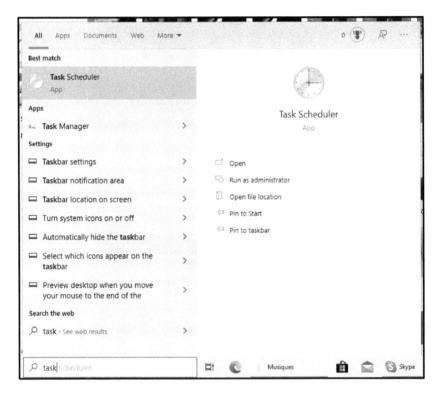

Figure 171: Write "task" in Windows, in the bottom left of your screen

Then click on "Create Task".

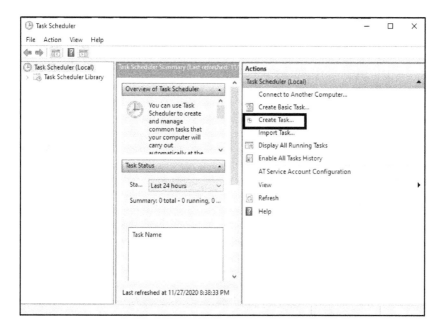

Figure 172: Task Scheduler screen

And give it a name like "SYNCHRO NAS":

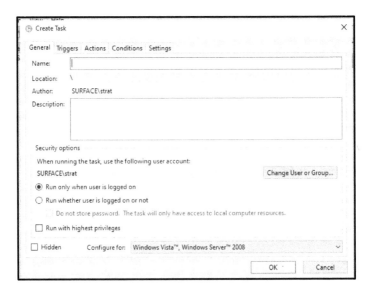

Figure 173: Task Setup Window

Then click on the "Actions" tab and click on the "New..." button.

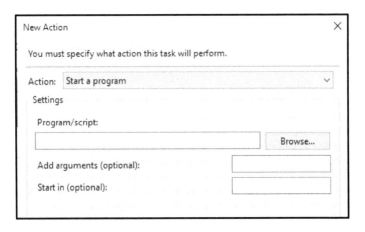

Figure 174: Modify Action

In "Program/script", enter:

"C:\Program Files\FreeFileSync.exe"

And in "Add arguments (optional)", enter:

"C:\Synchro\Settings.ffs_batch".

Click OK. Then go to the "Triggers" tab and click on "New..." and fill in the fields as shown in the example below:

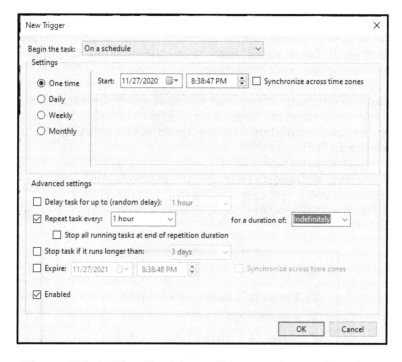

Figure 175: Setting the trigger. It seems strange, but since Windows 10, you have to set the task to "One time" even for a recurring task. Then check "Repeat task every..." + "for a duration of: Indefinitely"

Do not choose the same schedule for all computers in the family, so that the NAS is not overloaded with work. For example, set the sync of one computer at xx:00, another at xx:10, and another at xx:20. Since the sync is repeated every 30 minutes, they will also be at xx:30, xx:40, and xx:50.

Fill in the fields as shown in the screenshot above.

Click OK. Click OK again.

That's it, it's over.

From now on, every 30 minutes (or 1 hour or other frequency), there will be a small logo 🔄 in the taskbar (bottom right) indicating that synchronization is in progress.

Caution: Be patient because the first synchronization can take a very long time: an hour, a day, or even a week. It all depends on the amount of data and the speed of the network connection (slower in Wifi).

The execution reports (also called logs) explaining what has been synchronized can be found in the C:/Users/<folder>/AppData/Roaming/FreeFileSync/Logs folder.

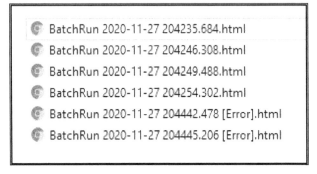

Figure 176: List of Implementation Reports

An execution report is used to indicate how each synchronization went. The file may contain the word "Warning" or "Error" in its name. This is a bad sign. In this case open the file and read the reason for the problem. Usually it is because one of the devices was not properly turned on or connected to the network and therefore the synchronization could not be performed normally.

MediaMonkey

https://www.mediamonkey.com

MediaMonkey is a very effective music playback software. It is free, fast, complete and pleasant to use.

After installing the software, launch it, then add your music to the Library by following the step below:

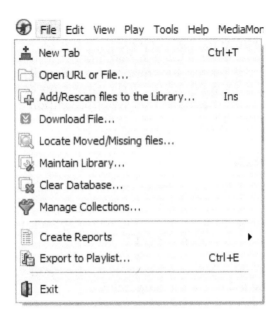

Figure 177: Choose "Add/Rescan Files to Library" menu

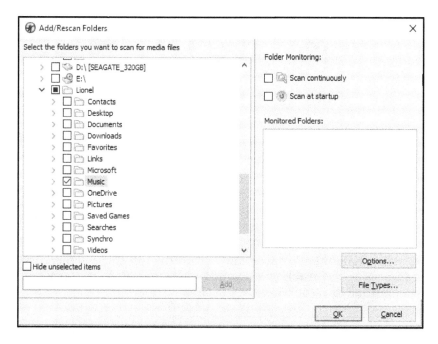

Figure 178: Select the folder(s) that contain your music

Now you can see all your MP3s in the main interface.

Navigate in the tree on the left, selecting artists, albums, years or genres.

Figure 179: Navigating through rap albums. The covers add a real added value: it is the digitization of the CD from A to Z.

With MediaMonkey's cover carousel at the top of the screen, you can choose the tracks you want to listen to, just as you would do manually in front of your CD shelf.

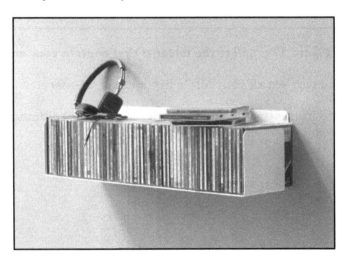

Figure 180: Remote memory

WinX DVD Ripper

https://www.winxdvd.com/dvd-ripper-platinum/index-fr.htm

WinX DVD Ripper is a paid software, capable of extracting any DVD video to convert it into a video file.

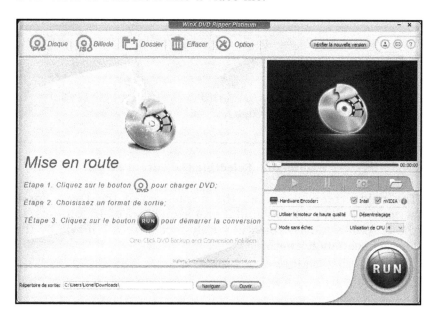

Figure 181: WinX DVD Ripper main screen

After launching the WinX DVD Ripper application, click the "Disc" button. A dialog box will propose several types of extraction files. Choose the "MP4 Video" format.

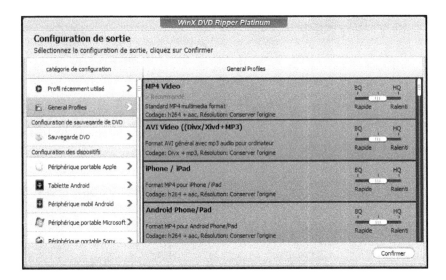

Figure 182: Selecting the output format

The next screen shows all the sequences of the DVD. For a series, you will probably find 3 or 4 sequences of 45 minutes. In the case of a movie, you will surely recognize the movie by the longest sequence length.

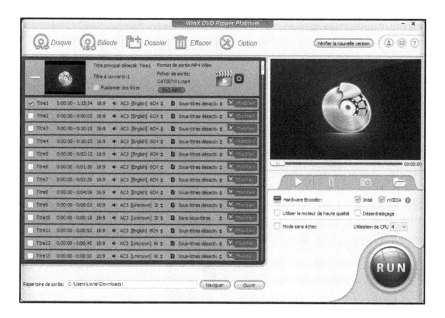

Figure 183: List of sequences

Remember to choose a language and a subtitle. Unlike the DVD, the MP4 file that will be produced will have only one language and one subtitle, so choose your options wisely.

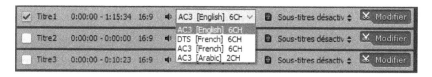

Figure 184: Language Choice

All you have to do is click on the big "RUN" button. It will take about half an hour to extract the film. The generated MP4 file can be found in the folder mentioned at the bottom of the window. The MP4 file is compatible with any hardware or software player and weighs between 650 megabytes and 1.7 gigabytes depending on the duration and quality of the picture.

SyncMe Wireless

https://play.google.com/store/apps/details?id=com.b
v.wifisync

SyncMe Wireless is an Android application that allows you to synchronize folders two by two: one being in the smartphone and the other accessible via a local network. If you own a NAS, SyncMe Wireless is the perfect application to eliminate the need for a USB cable.

Be very careful when configuring this tool: think carefully about the direction in which the synchronization is going to be done and choose well the mode of deletion repertories.

After installing and configuring SyncMe Wireless, you won't be one of those people who say "I'll have to back up what I have on my smartphone ... someday".

Launch the application. The first step of configuration is to enter the name of the NAS or its IP, and your account and password to access the NAS. This is information that you should already know.

The second step is to add a synchronization between two folders. In the "Add sync folder" menu, you will have to choose a "Device folder" i.e. an existing folder in the smartphone. Then you will have to choose a "Computer folder" i.e. an existing folder in the NAS. Very important: in "Schedule" you will choose the frequency at which the synchronizations should take place. For example, the synchronization can be done every day at half past midnight. At this time, you are very likely to be at home, and so is your smartphone.

Figure 185: Panel to connect to a NAS

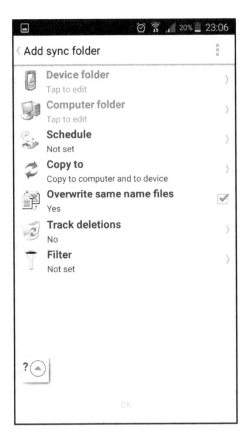

Figure 186: Synchro configuration panel

Also pay attention to the "Copy to" and "Track Deletions" settings.

"Copy to" is the parameter that will allow you to indicate the direction and nature of the synchronization.

- Bi-directional synchronization,
- Copy from smartphone to NAS,
- Copy from the NAS to the smartphone,

- Moving files from the smartphone to the NAS,
- Moving files from the NAS to the smartphone.

It is not recommended to synchronize with the "travel" modes. Copying leaves more room for backup in case of an incident.

The "Track Deletions" parameter is the one that allows you to choose the file deletion policy to be applied. Two behaviors are possible:

- Do not pass on deletions. This is an option that plays the card of caution. Once a file has been synchronized, it is permanent even if it is deleted in the source folder.
- Mirror deletions. With this option, folder B deletes all files that do not or no longer exist in folder A.

For example, to stream your MP3 collection from the NAS to your smartphone every day at one o'clock in the morning, choose the following options:

Device folder = The folder where your MP3s are in the smartphone.

Computer folder = The folder where your MP3s are stored in the NAS.

Schedule = "Run at 01:00".

Copy to = " Copy to device only ".

Track deletions = " Mirror " (Any MP3 deletion in your NAS will cause the same files to be deleted in your smartphone).

Second example, to send all the photos and videos you have taken during the day to your NAS, configure as follows:

Device folder = The folder where your photos and videos are stored in the smartphone.

Computer folder = A folder dedicated to photo backups, in your NAS.

Schedule = "Run at 23:00".

Copy to = " Copy to computer only ".

Track deletions = "No". Even if you delete your photos on your smartphone to make room, those that have already been saved on the NAS will remain there.

In both cases of use, if you are not at home at the time of synchronization, the synchronization will be in error and will display a small notification. It will start again the next day.

The main screen of the SyncMe Wireless application displays all the synchronizations, with the date and time of the last synchronization below each one and the number of files deleted (red) or added (blue).

The "Sync all" button at the bottom of the screen allows you to immediately start all synchronizations. It's almost magical: instead of getting a computer and a USB cable, you just touch this "Sync all" button and you exchange multiple files with your NAS.

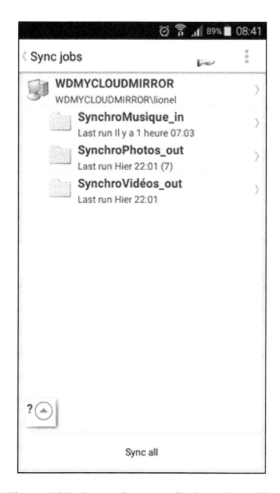

Figure 187: General screen listing all configured synchronizations

Don't hesitate to rename the syncs, for more readability, by touching the name of the sync, then " Edit " then " ⋮ " then " Rename ".

Ant Renamer

https://antp.be/software/renamer/fr

Ant Renamer is the reference for large file renaming. Its possibilities are countless.

The software takes the form of a very simple interface in which you can put files by drag and drop.

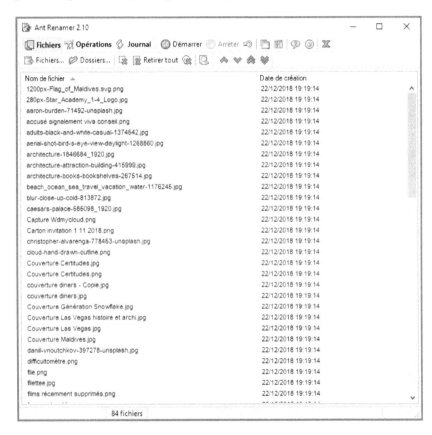

Figure 188: Ant Renamer's Main Screen

In the "Actions" tab, you can rename your files in more than a dozen ways. Let's take a first example. We want to rename a large number of photos simply based on their date and time:

Figure 189: Operation Tab - Date and Time

After clicking on "GO", we get this:

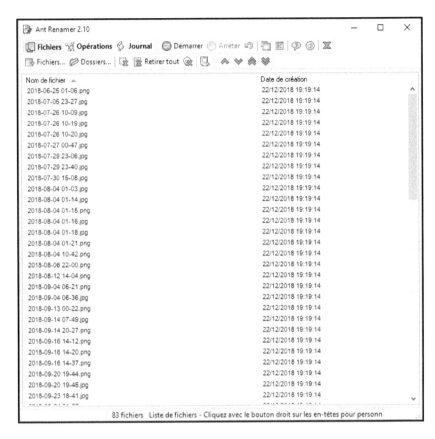

Figure 190: Main screen after modification

Second example: we want to add the name "Grand Canyon" in front of all the pictures we took there. We go to the "Actions" tab, and choose "String insertion".

Figure 191: Operations tab - Chain insertion

We fill in the word "Grand_Canyon_" in the string field to be inserted, as well as "At position 0" and from the beginning. And the renaming is done.

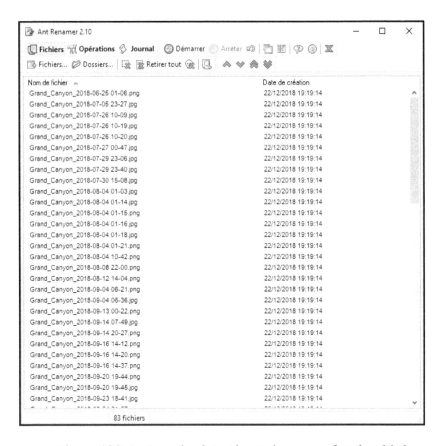

Figure 192: Let's go back to the main screen for the third time

For photos from iPhones or digital cameras, it can be interesting to change their name to use the date of the picture taken instead.

Let's take for example these 4 photo files taken by an iPhone:

Nom	Prise de vue
IMG_6016.JPEG	03/11/2020 08:39
IMG_5613.JPEG	29/08/2020 13:12
IMG_5214.JPEG	01/08/2020 16:09
IMG_5183.JPEG	01/08/2020 12:59

Figure 193: Their name is abstruse while their shooting date is filled in.

You have to rename with the "EXIF Info" function of Ant Renamer as below. Write %datetime%%ext% in the parameter on the right.

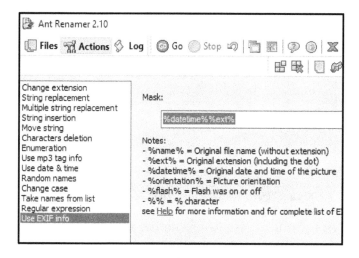

Figure 194: Renaming function with date of capture

Nom	Prise de vue
2020-11-03 08-39-33.JPG	03/11/2020 08:39
2020-08-29 13-12-22.JPG	29/08/2020 13:12
2020-08-01 16-09-59.JPG	01/08/2020 16:09
2020-08-01 12-59-38.JPG	01/08/2020 12:59

Figure 195: Renamed files

It is also possible to add a description at the end, for example:

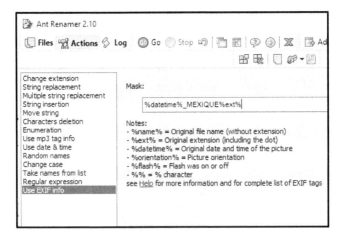

Figure 196: Renaming with shot and place name

Even better, you can ask Ant Renamer to add the folder name at the end of the file name. This allows you to rename several files located in several different folders. Take a look at this example:

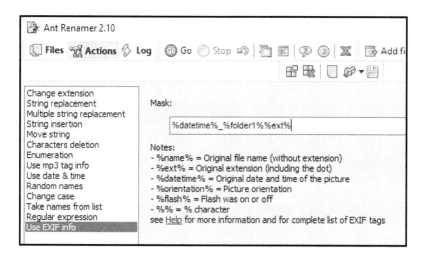

Figure 197: Renaming with shot and folder name

Nom de fichier ⌃

2020-08-01 12-59-38_Voyage à Cuba.JPG

2020-08-01 16-09-59_Voyage à Cuba.JPG

2020-08-29 13-12-22_Naissance de Kévin.JPG

2020-11-03 08-39-33_Voyage à Cuba.JPG

2020-08-01 15-37-04_Mariage de Steve et Elsa.JPEG

2020-08-01 15-37-06_Voyage à Cuba.JPEG

2020-08-01 16-06-53_Voyage à Cuba.JPEG

2020-08-01 16-06-54_Mariage de Steve et Elsa.JPEG

2020-08-01 16-06-57_Mariage de Steve et Elsa.JPEG

2020-08-01 16-09-56_Mariage de Steve et Elsa.JPEG

2020-08-01 16-09-57_Mariage de Steve et Elsa.JPEG

2020-08-01 16-09-59_Mariage de Steve et Elsa.JPEG

2020-08-01 16-10-01_Mariage de Steve et Elsa.JPEG

2020-08-01 21-01-02_Mariage de Steve et Elsa.JPEG

Figure 198Result of the previous share

Overcoming digital mess | 203

Of course, you can also reverse the order, if you want, with %folder1%_%datetime%%ext% instead of %datetime%_%folder1%%ext%.

```
Nom de fichier  ▼
Voyage à Cuba_2020-11-03 08-39-33.JPG
Voyage à Cuba_2020-08-01 16-09-59.JPG
Voyage à Cuba_2020-08-01 16-06-53.JPEG
Voyage à Cuba_2020-08-01 15-37-06.JPEG
Voyage à Cuba_2020-08-01 12-59-38.JPG
Naissance de Kévin_2020-08-29 13-12-22.JPG
Mariage de Steve et Elsa_2020-08-01 21-01-02.JPEG
Mariage de Steve et Elsa_2020-08-01 16-10-01.JPEG
Mariage de Steve et Elsa_2020-08-01 16-09-59.JPEG
Mariage de Steve et Elsa_2020-08-01 16-09-57.JPEG
Mariage de Steve et Elsa_2020-08-01 16-09-56.JPEG
Mariage de Steve et Elsa_2020-08-01 16-06-57.JPEG
Mariage de Steve et Elsa_2020-08-01 16-06-54.JPEG
Mariage de Steve et Elsa_2020-08-01 15-37-04.JPEG
```

Figure 199: Renaming reverse. But it is less advisable to put away your photos. Chronological order is a common rule.

Ant Rename also offers:

- To rename file extensions,
- Replace one word by another (useful if you have misspelled the same word on hundreds of files),
- To delete characters,
- To list the files,
- To choose random names,
- To change everything to upper or lower case,
- etc.

CDex

https://cdex.mu/

CDex is a very well-known freeware. It is used to extract music from an audio CD. Very easy to use, just put the audio CD in your computer's drive, then enter the artist's name and song titles on the keyboard. All that remains is to select all the pieces you want to extract and press F9. Then you have to wait for about one minute per piece.

Each piece of music produces an MP3 file located in the "Music" folder. Rename it and store it somewhere else if you wish.

Remember that it is forbidden to distribute MP3s. Out of respect for copyright, you have the right to copy a CD as long as the MP3s remain only in devices that belong to you.

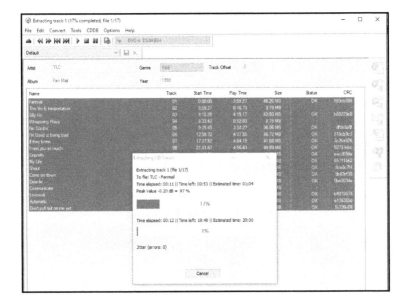

Figure 200: Music extraction with CDex

Synthesis

This book has tried to help you overcome the digital accumulation syndrome. The avalanche of files, applications, USB sticks, CDs, DVDs, external disks, SD cards, tablets, smartphones that surround us has ended up suffocating those who have not taken adequate measures.

There are three zones of presence of your files:

- The **offline zone** which is composed of all non-communicating media such as cameras, USB sticks, memory cards and optical disks.

- The **online zone,** which is made up of all devices connected to the network but which are not intended to centralize data: smartphones, tablets and personal computers. These are the devices we have in front of us all day long.

- And finally, the **central zone** which is composed of media such as the cloud or NAS.

Throughout the pages, we have seen that the objective is to entrust all our files to the central zone and to empty the offline zone as much as possible. The online zone needs to arbitrate between terminal mode and synchronized mode on a case-by-case basis, but under no circumstances should it have unsaved files.

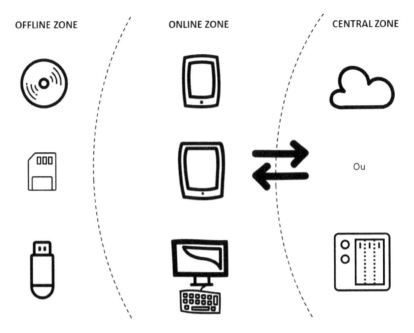

Figure 201: The three zones where your files are located

Nevertheless, the growing disaffection of users for files will eventually solve the problem by itself. The file, which is too technical a concept, is giving way to video on demand or streaming. MP3s have given way to Spotify, YouTube or Deezer. DVDs and CDs have also been replaced.

A close relationship between smartphone and cloud also sent the PC to the brink.

However, users who continue to operate in file mode can rely on a few reflexes and several tools to put their digital life in order.

Your files are arranged, sorted, renamed. Your old media have been digitized. Your attachments are archived. Everything is centralized on a device accessible online. Congratulations, you have overcome the digital mess.

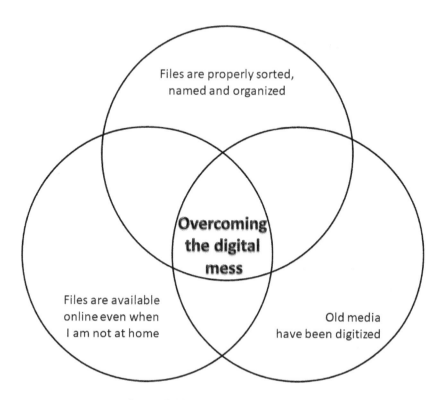

Files are properly sorted, named and organized

Overcoming the digital mess

Files are available online even when I am not at home

Old media have been digitized

Figure 202: Overcoming Digital Mess

Conclusion

The lifestyle that we have gradually learned as we grow up encourages us to eat well, play sports or tidy up our home. But the one consisting in tidying up our files has escaped us until now. Seen as a waste of time, it proves to be creative and precisely saves future time by highlighting past time, pleasant or unpleasant memories, twirling at the whim of the 4G in a phone thirty years younger than the files it displays. It's a time of ubiquity and omnipresence: all the devices I touch become the same, because, one password away, the user that I am is always in front of the same universe located in a small box hidden in his home or in the immensity of large cabinets jealously guarded by a hosting company.

Files are knowledge, they are leisure, pleasure, memory, indispensable, administrative, obligatory, rescue. Every day they write a part of us, they describe a part of ourselves.

Sources

Wikipedia page of " Computer files "
https://fr.wikipedia.org/wiki/Fichier_informatique

Wikipedia page of " Punch Card "
https://fr.wikipedia.org/wiki/Carte_perfor%C3%A9e

Wikipedia page for "Microsoft Word".
https://fr.wikipedia.org/wiki/Microsoft_Word

Wikipedia page of " Hard Disk "
https://fr.wikipedia.org/wiki/Disque_dur

Wikipedia page of " Floppy disk "
https://fr.wikipedia.org/wiki/Disquette

Wikipedia page of "Super 8".
https://fr.wikipedia.org/wiki/Super_8

Illustration icons
https://www.iconfinder.com

Illustration icons
https://www.flaticon.com/

Illustration photos
https://www.pexels.com

Article " How To Organize Your Messy Windows Desktop (And
Keep It That Way) " article
https://www.howtogeek.com/362241/how-to-organize-your-
messy-windows-desktop-and-keep-it-that-way/

Wikipedia page of " ID3 (MP3 metadata)

https://fr.wikipedia.org/wiki/ID3_(m%C3%A9tadonn%C3%A9es_MP3)

Page " St. Ghislain, Belgium " from Google Data Centers
https://www.google.com/about/datacenters/inside/locations/st-ghislain/

Photo of a data center
https://www.businesswire.com/news/home/20190627005990/en/NTT-Com-Develops-the-Largest-Data-Center-in-Indonesia

WinX DVD Ripper Platinum website
https://www.winxdvd.com

Article "List of the best Mac synchronization software".
https://www.sync-mac.com/fr/list-of-mac-synchronization-software.html

Amazon Drive website
https://www.amazon.fr/clouddrive/home

Google Drive website
https://drive.google.com/

OneDrive website
https://onedrive.live.com/about/fr-fr/

Dropbox website
https://www.dropbox.com/fr/

SFR Cloud website
https://www.sfrcloud.sfr.fr/

Article " Small Business Backup: Where to Backup Data " Article
https://www.novabackup.com/blog/small-business-where-to-backup-data

Western Digital website

https://www.wd.com/fr-fr/products/portable-storage/my-passport-wireless-ssd.html

Book " Backup your files " by Lionel Bolnet
http://www.lulu.com/shop/lionel-bolnet/sauvegarder-ses-fichiers/paperback/product-23225404.html

Site kevin-group.com
http://kevin-group.com/3-3ft-premium-quality-3-in-1-multiple-usb-charging-cable-with-8-pin-lighting-micro-usb-type-c-for-iphone-6s-6-6-plus-5-5s-5c-galaxy-s3-4-nexus-6p-more/

Book " How to use your My Cloud Mirror " by Lionel Bolnet
http://www.lulu.com/shop/lionel-bolnet/bien-utiliser-son-my-cloud-mirror/paperback/product-22948112.html

Article "1,000 billion photos have been taken thanks to smartphones".
https://fr.businessam.be/en-2017-1000-milliards-de-photos-ont-ete-prises-grace-aux-smartphones/#:~:text=R%C3%A9result%2C%20the esp%C3%A8ce%20human%20a,take%205%20photos%20by%20Oday.

Article "Graduation thesis: a student gets her work stolen and calls for help".
https://mcetv.fr/mon-mag-campus/memoire-fin-etudes-etudiante-fait-voler-appelle-aide-2504/

World Backup Day website
http://www.worldbackupday.com/fr/

Article " Having your laptop stolen is traumatic. Here's what I learned"
https://www.theguardian.com/technology/2015/jan/20/laptop-stolen-what-i-learned

The Author

Lionel Bolnet is a French computer engineer and writer born on July 14, 1984.

He is also the author of:

- Understanding Sybase ASE 15.7,
- Backup your files,
- The Maldives.

For more information, visit:

`http://www.lulu.com/spotlight/lbolnet.`